SOCCEROOS
IN SCOTLAND

SOCCEROOS
IN SCOTLAND

PAUL MURPHY

FAIRPLAY
PUBLISHING

First published in 2025 by Fair Play Publishing

PO Box 4101, Balgowlah Heights, NSW 2093, Australia
www.fairplaypublishing.com.au

ISBN: 978-1-923236-29-5
ISBN: 9778-1-923236-30-1

© Paul Murphy 2025

The moral rights of the author have been asserted.
All rights reserved. Except as permitted under the *Australian Copyright Act 1968* (for example, a fair dealing for the purposes of study, research, criticism or review), no part of this book may be reproduced, stored in a retrieval system, communicated or transmitted in any form or by any means without prior written permission from the Publisher.

Design and typesetting by Leslie Priestley
Front cover: Mark Viduka (Celtic) and Craig Johnston (Rangers) by Alamy
Back Cover: Ange Postecoglou Ange Postecoglou with one of the three trophies he won as manager of Celtic, the Scottish League Cup against Hibernian, 2021 by Alamy
Other photographs: Alamy, David Bell/Tontastic, Fair Play Collection, Will Hastie, Danny Invincibile

A catalogue record of this book is available from the National Library of Australia.

Contents

Introduction		1
Chapter 1	The Pioneer: Dave Mitchell	4
Chapter 2	The Ones Who Didn't Make It	12
Chapter 3	The Breakthrough Star	32
Chapter 4	"You're Staying With Us Now"	42
Chapter 5	The One-Season Wonder	53
Chapter 6	The Agent	60
Chapter 7	The Star Striker	67
Chapter 8	The Standby Socceroo	82
Chapter 9	Adventures in Gretna and Greenock	92
Chapter 10	The Football Fashionista	102
Chapter 11	Magic Moments: Tom Rogic	108
Chapter 12	Aussies in Leith	121
Chapter 13	Aussie Blood, Edinburgh Hearts	128
Chapter 14	The Late Developer	137
Chapter 15	The Boss	144
Chapter 16	From a Trickle to a Flood	159

Introduction

When I was growing up in Scotland in the 1980s, Australia held a certain exotic and glamorous appeal. Its geographical distance meant it was unlikely that most Scots would ever travel there, never mind live in the country. However, it didn't seem uncommon to hear of friends with cousins there, and every so often one of your school classmates would emigrate to the other side of the world.

Australia's attractions were clear. Your friend would show you pictures of the house his cousins lived in. As you resided in a semi-detached three-bedroom house with a small garden in the suburbs, emigrating to Perth or Brisbane or Melbourne seemed to bring the guarantee of a five-bedroom villa, with a sprawling garden for regular barbecues and a swimming pool. And, in contrast with Glasgow or Edinburgh, the sun always seemed to be shining.

Then there was the increasing influence of Australian popular culture on the psyche. Scotland may have given Australia AC/DC, but the 80s brought *Mad Max*, INXS and *Crocodile Dundee* to Scotland and the wider world. The bright and photogenic young stars of *Neighbours* and *Home and Away* became unlikely teen idols—a far cry from the austere period drama of the previous decade, *The Sullivans*. If the 90s brought the concept of Cool Britannia, the 80s was the decade of 'Cool Australia'. Why would anyone wish to swap a life there for a life under the grey skies of Scotland?

The Aussies were good at sport, too. Pat Cash won Wimbledon, the rugby and cricket teams were always strong, and that Greg Norman was a decent golfer.

But when it came to Scotland's most popular sport, well, Australia just didn't seem to have much going for it back then. Everyone knew of Craig Johnston as he played for the all-conquering Liverpool side, but apart from him, Australian footballers were an unknown quantity.

Before the 1980s, the trend was very much to migrate north to south, and that was also true for football players.

Great Britain's colonisation of Australia had resulted in the first significant numbers of Scots moving to Australia in the 19th century. Records from the ScotlandsPeople website report that almost 5,000 people from Scotland's Highlands and Islands emigrated to Australia between 1852 and 1857 "in search of a better life". Many thousands would follow over the next century and more—sometimes as a result of extreme poverty, and sometimes just to look for a better standard of living than that offered by the somewhat grim conditions of some of Scotland's towns and cities in the late 19th and early 20th centuries.

It is not difficult to find the influence of Scotland on Australian society in general, and that includes the development of its football. One look at the list of Australian caps shows many to be Scottish-born and/or raised. Cap No.1—Alec Gibb—grew up just outside Edinburgh. Gibb was one of four Scots named in Australia's first-ever national squad in 1922.

There was a strong Scottish influence in the Australia side that made it to the country's first-ever World Cup finals in 1974. They had Jimmy Mackay to thank for taking them there, as his goal against South Korea secured qualification. That is still one of the most iconic goals in Aussie football history. The Edinburgh man was selected alongside two fellow Scots turned Aussies—goalkeeper Jack Reilly and winger Jimmy Rooney.

Just over a decade on, the Socceroos met Scotland in a playoff for a place at the 1986 World Cup. Kenny Murphy and Joe Watson had grown up in the country of their birth and were now playing against them, while teammates Robbie Dunn and Dave Mitchell were also Scots-born, though had moved to Australia at an early age. On the touchline, former Hearts defender Eddie Thomson was the Socceroos assistant coach. Thomson would go on to become the manager in the following decade.

So it was clear that from the very first days of football in Australia, Scotland had a significant influence all the way up until the mid-1980s. And then, the trend started to reverse. Slowly at first. Very slowly. In the mid to late 1990s, it gathered momentum and in the 2020s, the Aussie influence on Scottish football is stronger than ever.

From the 1980s to the 2000s, the quality of Australian football players caught up with and, at least temporarily, surpassed Scotland's. For many of Australia's finest, Scotland would be either a stopping-off point or a place that became home for the best part of 10 years.

The trend for Australians to leave their home shores had started to gather pace in the 1990s and when the country qualified for just its second World Cup in 2006, the 23-man squad had only three home-based players. None of them were playing in Scotland at the time, though Craig Moore and Mark Viduka had certainly made their names there.

It actually took until 2018 for the Aussies to feature any Scotland-based players in their World Cup squad. Celtic's Tom Rogic and Hibernian's Jamie Maclaren were the pair that year, though the squad also included Jackson Irvine and Aaron Mooy, who had previously played in Scotland and would do so again. And then came the 2022 World Cup squad and its abundance of Scotland-Australia links.

Such was the relationship between Scottish football and Australian football that the Socceroos squad for the 2022 World Cup had no fewer than 10 direct connections. Six were playing in the Scottish Premiership at the time, while four others had previously played in that league. Two more would be added to the list of Socceroos in Scotland the following year. When Australia lined up against Lionel Messi's Argentina in the 2022 World Cup, the starting XI included Dundee United's Aziz Behich, Scottish-born and raised Harry Souttar, Hearts' Kye Rowles, Celtic's Aaron Mooy and St Mirren's Keanu Baccus. Players on the bench included Hearts' Cammy Devlin and Nathaniel Atkinson, as well as Jason Cummings, another player who had previously spent most of his life as a Scot.

This book takes a look at how, in the space of 40 years, Australians in Scottish football went from being a novelty to becoming a regular feature. There are exclusive interviews with some of the Australian players who have graced the top level of the Scottish game since Dave Mitchell got the ball rolling back in 1983. It not only features a look at some of the biggest stars, but it also tells stories of those who didn't quite succeed and some who had relatively modest careers.

CHAPTER 1
The Pioneer: Dave Mitchell

In the early 1980s, Scotland's football demographic was a world away from the multinational modern game. Squads tended to be at least 90 percent Scottish, and it wasn't unusual for them to have 100 percent homegrown talents.

Another significant difference was in the competitive nature of the game. Titles were won by Aberdeen, Celtic and Dundee United between 1979 and 1983. Rangers were generally fourth best.

It was this environment that Dave Mitchell entered when he swapped Sydney for Glasgow, returning to the city of his birth after growing up in South Australia. More importantly for his family, he was joining the club that his father loved.

While the connection to Rangers was clear, it was still somewhat surprising to see the Gers look to the other side of the globe for a player to help lift them after a difficult four seasons in which they had failed to mount a serious title challenge, never mind become champions.

If there were players from outside the country in a Scottish Premier League squad, they tended to be from one of the immediate neighbours in the British Isles. In 1983, Rangers had Jimmy Nicholl and John McClelland from Northern Ireland, and the more exotic Robert Prytz from Sweden. The rest of the squad were Scots until a lone Australian international striker added another nationality to the mix.

In even more parochial times, Australia was a genuine footballing outpost, both in geographical terms and in terms of its quality of play. The only recognisable Aussie footballer at the time was Liverpool's Craig Johnston, while Scotland could still boast several world-class players and a strong league on the European stage. Aberdeen, led in those days by Alex Ferguson, had beaten both Bayern Munich and Real Madrid to lift the European Cup Winners' Cup in

1983, but ended the domestic season in third spot, behind Dundee United and Celtic. Rangers were back in fourth—17 points adrift of Aberdeen when a victory won you just two points.

So, the question on many fans' lips was, "Why Dave Mitchell?" This was the story of someone who was determined to make it happen. Mitchell had aspirations far beyond the domestic league in the footballing outpost of his adopted country.

He was no stranger to the international stage, having starred in the FIFA World Youth Championship in 1981. The tournament was hosted in Mitchell's native Australia and his team acquitted themselves well, making it past the group stage before being narrowly beaten by eventual winners West Germany in the quarter-final.

In that group stage, the Aussies went unbeaten, drawing 3–3 with Cameroon and 1–1 with an England side that featured future stars Paul Allen, Stewart Robson and Neil Webb. The highlight was undoubtedly a stirring 2–1 victory over Argentina. Their opponents in that match had Jorge Burruchaga in their lineup—the player who went on to score the winning goal in the 1986 World Cup final.

This experience may have whetted Mitchell's appetite but finding his way out of the limits of the Australian game would not be easy. Determined to make it happen, he was even prepared to pay a significant chunk of money to give himself a shot at the club from his city of birth.

First, he had to get the club's attention, and luck had it that his father, Jimmy, had played at semi-professional level alongside Stan Anderson, who had become assistant to Rangers manager John Greig. Mitchell's dad wrote to Anderson, enclosed a load of newspaper clippings about his son's achievements to date and indicated that he was a player very much in demand.

Greig was happy to have a look, which was significant in itself. Greig was arguably the club's greatest-ever player at that time. He had helped the club to considerable domestic success in the mid-1960s before Celtic took over as the country's leading side. However, Greig stayed around long enough for the pendulum to swing back towards Ibrox, the home of Rangers. He captained the the Gers to domestic trebles in 1976 and 1978, and, perhaps most memorably, he was skipper when Rangers lifted the European Cup Winners' Cup in 1972.

Having got Greig's attention, Mitchell went for a three-month trial at Ibrox. Unfortunately, the trial took place during a particularly harsh winter that limited opportunities to show what he could do, with training forced indoors on many occasions due to the frozen pitches.

What Greig did see impressed him, but he was not prepared to pay the AUD 100,000 that Mitchell's club Adelaide City wanted. Sydney City would, however, pay significantly less to take him east to New South Wales. The fee was $35,000—an Australian record at the time.

The dream of playing for Rangers would not die, though, and following a successful, title-winning year at Sydney, Mitchell pushed for a move again. But Sydney City wanted their money back, having invested such a significant fee in the young player. At just 21, Mitchell stumped up $30,000 to buy out his contract and seal a deal with the Gers as a free agent. It was a huge gamble that reflected the confidence he had in his ability to make an impact in the Scottish Premier League at a club that was crying out for a hero who would lift the team after several years of mediocrity.

Australian sports journalist Jason Dasey recalls how Mitchell's move to Rangers was received in his home country: "I remember first seeing Dave playing for Australia in the FIFA World Youth Championship in 1981. He was one of the outstanding players in the tournament and Australia did very well.

"I always followed his career after that. In the old National Soccer League, he was one of the top players, and I think he won Young Player of the Year. But while he was becoming a star in the domestic league, he had a dream of playing overseas and had to gamble by paying a significant sum of money to terminate his contract.

"$30,000 AUS was a huge amount of money at the time. Dave was so broke that he had to fly over on someone else's air ticket. In those days, security wasn't so tight. He was flying with a friend of the person whose ticket it was, so he had to pretend he was with this woman he didn't really know.

"He ended up making it all the way to the UK, flying on someone else's ticket. It was huge news at the time because the only Australian player who had really broken through on a big international stage was Craig Johnston at Middlesbrough and then Liverpool. It was the early stages of a lot of Aussies going to Europe, and Dave was certainly a pioneer."

In hindsight, the gamble paid off. Mitchell offered something a little different at a time when strikers tended to fall into one of two categories: big target man or shorter 'fox-in-the-box' types. In an interview with *SBS Sport*, Mitchell said, "I was a big and quick striker and quite aggressive. But I reckon I had more technical ability than many people would give me credit for."

His stay at Rangers would have a promising beginning, but there would be no fairytale ending, in contrast to his strike partner on the day of his competitive debut. A goal in a League Cup tie at Queen of the South was a positive start for Mitchell. Also on the scoresheet that day was Ally McCoist, the player who would go on to become arguably Rangers' greatest-ever striker.

Both players started again the following week in a fixture with a much higher profile. Mitchell was thrown into the league match at Celtic Park, in front of an official crowd of over 50,000. The young Australian's performance on the biggest stage of his career to date was so impressive that he was named man of the match.

The outcome of the game was ultimately disappointing, however. McCoist had Rangers ahead in 30 seconds, but the home side eventually prevailed, with a late goal sealing a 2-1 victory. Even so, the first Australian in the top tier of Scottish football had hit the ground running and earned the trust of his manager in one of world football's biggest derby matches. The following week, Mitchell would net his first league goal, though it came in another defeat—this time a 3-1 loss away to Hearts.

The first goals at Ibrox came in a 10-0 victory over Maltese side Valletta in the Cup Winners' Cup, and he would score against Porto in the same tournament a few weeks later. Mitchell was developing a taste for the big European nights. His star was very much on the rise.

Looking back, Dasey felt that Mitchell adapted quickly because his skill set was perfectly suited to the Scottish game: "Dave looked like a classic No. 9 in some ways. He was a big guy, about 6ft1in, and he was good in the air. But he was also very proud of his dribbling ability, and he had electrifying pace. He didn't like it when he was just dismissed as a typical big, physical centre-forward.

"He was definitely more technically skilled than some of the strikers of that era. He could play as part of a front two or as a lone striker.

"You have to remember that, as a young man, he had been playing for a few years against older, seasoned professionals in Australia, so by the time he reached Scotland, he was ready for the challenge."

If it had been a decent start for the Australian at an individual level, his team was struggling domestically. A 3-0 defeat at home to St Mirren was the final straw. John Greig, the manager who had brought him to Rangers, was fired. Mitchell would have to prove himself all over again. Just a few months into his career in Scotland, his dream move was in danger of turning sour.

Who knows how things may have turned out had Aberdeen boss Alex Ferguson accepted Rangers' offer to replace Greig. Who knows what may have happened if Dundee United manager Jim McClean had taken over instead of Jock Wallace.

But the former boss was back, and Wallace's return to Ibrox followed very public rejections from Scotland's two brightest managers. Perhaps this was the moment that Mitchell's longer-term fate was sealed.

Wallace brought in Bobby Williamson to play striker, and Mitchell scored just one league goal under the new manager that season. The Australian did net a crucial goal in a 1-1 draw in the first leg of the League Cup semi-final at Dundee United in February 1984. Rangers made sure of a place in the final with a 2-0 home victory, but Mitchell was not in the squad for the final when a McCoist hat trick saw the Ibrox side lift the trophy with a 3-2 win over Celtic after extra time.

The bruising physical presences of Sandy Clark and Colin McAdam in the squad at Hampden Park was perhaps a clear indication of Wallace's preferences. Mitchell may have been able to hold his own in any physical confrontation, but Clark and McAdam were very much typical battling strikers who riled up opposing defenders.

Mitchell continued to play a bit-part role for much of the following season, but it wasn't without its highlights. He lifted a winner's medal in the League Cup final after coming on as a substitute in a 1-0 win over Dundee United.

One particularly memorable moment came when he scored in a 3-1 victory over a star-studded Inter Milan in the UEFA Cup. This was an Inter side that featured the legendary Giuseppe Bergomi in defence, former Arsenal and Republic of Ireland hero Liam Brady in midfield, and a strike pairing of Alessandro Altobelli and Karl-Heinz Rummenigge. Unfortunately, Rangers would go out 4-3 on aggregate, having been defeated 3-0 in Italy, but there was a spirited performance in the home leg.

It seemed that Mitchell might finally be finding favour with Jock Wallace, and he soon went on a run of four goals in seven league matches between mid-November and late December 1984.

But by this point, further competition had been added to the squad in the shape of Iain Ferguson up front and Ted McMinn on the wing. In another indication of Wallace's fondness for the big target man, he brought Derek

Johnstone back to Rangers in January 1985. That same month, Mitchell made his final appearance for the club in a 3-1 Scottish Cup win over Morton. He signed off with a goal.

Frustratingly, Mitchell was out of favour when the team was not delivering on the pitch. It just seemed clear that his face would not fit, and he started to look elsewhere. Playing in front of a full Ibrox Stadium on European nights had convinced him that his career would benefit from a move to a new environment. He felt that his playing style would perhaps be better suited to the more possession-based football played in other European countries.

In 2022, he told the *Daily Mail*, "It was a very difficult period to be at Rangers. Aberdeen were the kings and you had Dundee United as well. Alex Ferguson and Jim McLean built really good teams and Celtic and Rangers were fighting it out to be next.

"Jock Wallace returned as manager in 1983 and he wanted his own players. I played against Inter Milan and had a great game, scored against Porto and did quite well.

"I was in and out of the team. I wanted to go and play in Europe because I felt the football they played in Europe was much better. Rangers were stuck in their traditions and it stifled it a little bit for the players.

"You had to wear a shirt and tie to training, you had to be clean shaven, you couldn't do this and couldn't do that. Some of the methods were a bit antiquated and the club had to move forward."

Just as Mitchell's arrival at Rangers followed a tricky contractual situation, his exit also required negotiating some tricky hurdles. Such was the nature of his contract, a return to Sydney City was not an option as it would have given them back control of his career. Mitchell's contract at Rangers stipulated that any move to another British club would require a transfer fee, which could have proved an unwanted barrier. In order to avoid any complications further down the line and become a free agent again, Mitchell joined Seiko Sports Association in Hong Kong on a short-term deal.

Rangers fans might have been surprised by his choice of club, but he was to play under George Knobel, former manager of Ajax and the Dutch national side. And one of his teammates in Hong Kong was two-time World Cup finalist Rene van de Kerhof. This brief but enjoyable stay in East Asia allowed Mitchell to lift some silverware as Seiko sealed the Hong Kong title in his time there.

There was always a method to Mitchell's career moves and at 23, as a free agent once more, he went on to make a name for himself in Germany with Eintracht Frankfurt. An interesting twist of fate then brought Mitchell back to Glasgow in the same year that he had left Ibrox.

In November 1985, Scotland hosted Australia in a two-legged playoff to decide which of these two countries would qualify for the 1986 World Cup in Mexico. Mitchell stood out among his teammates. He was the one with the biggest pedigree, as the first Australian to play in the Scottish Premier League and then the Bundesliga. With the exception of Oscar Crino, who played in Cyprus, the rest of the Socceroos' lineup was made up of players from the National Soccer League.

Meanwhile, under the temporary leadership of Alex Ferguson (appointed after the tragic death of Jock Stein following a World Cup qualifier against Wales in September 1985), the Scots could call upon seven players who had won European trophies with either Liverpool or Aberdeen. They included Graeme Souness, Kenny Dalglish and Gordon Strachan. Scotland were obviously clear favourites and it was Mitchell's former Rangers teammate Davie Cooper who broke the Hampden Park deadlock with a brilliant free kick before Frank McAvennie added a second to seal a 2–0 victory for the hosts.

It took a determined performance from the Aussies to keep the scoreline down despite the gaps in quality, and they gave as good as they got in the return leg in Melbourne two weeks later. Scotland were happy to settle for a 0–0 draw to ensure qualification, but it was another indication that Australia, with Mitchell at the forefront, were improving as a footballing nation.

In a post-match interview following the second leg, Ferguson expressed his dissatisfaction with the Scotland performance and noted how hard it had been for his side to deal with Australia's physical approach.

Ferguson said, "It's great to get there (the World Cup), but I just wish we had played better. In the first half in particular, we gave them too many opportunities to play the ball into our penalty box, which they were going to enjoy, making it a fighting game, a battle, with aerial contact all the time. In the circumstances, our defenders did really well and our goalkeeper did well. It's not the kind of game you like to see in international football, but that's what they're strong at."

It was perhaps a slightly condescending view of an underdog that had put up a good fight, but in the days before social media introduced the concept of the farmers' league, it was an indication of how Australian football was viewed at the time.

After his time at Eintracht was up, Mitchell would go on to star in the Netherlands with Feyenoord, and his career also featured brief spells at Chelsea and Newcastle United.

Things perhaps hadn't worked out as hoped at Rangers but Mitchell had lived the dream, played in some big matches and scored against two of Europe's top sides.

He hadn't gone to Scotland as a launch pad to bigger things in better leagues. At that time, Rangers was the dream destination. As it turned out, it was an interesting chapter in what would become a very colourful career for several big clubs and his country. He had not played for a vintage Rangers side, but at least he had played for the club supported by his family.

He had also made history as the first Australian in the Scottish Premier League, paving the way for many who would follow in his footsteps.

After significant financial investment in the club, Rangers finally became the dominant force in Scottish football again. Under Graeme Souness, and then Walter Smith, they left behind the mediocrity of the early 1980s as they became very much the top side in the country in the 1990s.

For a brief moment, it looked like Mitchell might make a surprise return to Ibrox to join a club that was in a very different place than it had been when he first joined a decade earlier.

After Mitchell had helped Swindon Town win promotion to the English Premier League under Glenn Hoddle in 1993, Rangers boss Walter Smith looked into bringing the now 31-year-old Aussie back to the club. It was a move that appealed to Mitchell, but this time he couldn't make it happen.

It made no difference to his legacy, however. Mitchell had already made his mark as one of the early pioneers of Australian football.

CHAPTER 2
The Ones Who Didn't Make It

Will Hastie

"I remember the day Tommy Craig asked me to come into his office. Cesar—Big Billy McNeill—was sitting there, and they said they had received an offer for me from Dundee and that they would like me to take that offer.

"I asked if it was a loan, but they said that they wanted to release me to have the opportunity to play for Dundee. I was on my own at the time, and I was still only 18 years old. It was pretty confronting. I remember my lip quivering and saying that I didn't want to go to Dundee. If I was going to be 12,000 miles away from home, I only wanted to be at Celtic.

"They just repeated that they were releasing me, along with several other players that day. I didn't say anything else because I just didn't know what to say. There was a legend like Billy in the room, and I remember turning around, leaving the room, and walking around the red ash track that went around the pitch at Celtic Park in tears. I did a couple of laps like that, and I didn't know what was going to come next."

If Dave Mitchell's time at Rangers seemed like a breakthrough for Australian players, a few more would fall short in the years ahead. Will Hastie had gone to Scotland to represent his country in 1989 and ended up signing a deal at the club he had supported since childhood. But, as was the case for a few young Aussies around this time, there was to be no happy ending.

Hastie was on Celtic's radar due to the influence of one of the many Scots who had made his name in Australian football, and it did seem that a dream was about to come true.

Hastie recalled, "I got selected for the Australian U16 team that was in the 1989 World Cup in Scotland. An expat Scottish footballer called Hammy McMeechan, who is a legend locally from his time with Melbourne Croatia, was close with Tommy Burns [one of Celtic's most decorated and popular players of the 1970s and 1980s].

"He had written to Tommy and had let him know that I would be over, so some scouts kept an eye on the three games we played in the tournament. Unfortunately, we went out in the group stages. But they had seen enough to offer me a trial at Parkhead and I never ended up going home from that tournament. I had my trial and I signed a contract, which was a two-year YTS (Youth Training Scheme) deal."

This was quite the contrast with the arduous journey made by Mitchell who had opted to make significant financial sacrifices to buy himself out of contracts to earn a deal with the team on the other side of the city. It seemed so much easier for Hastie. However, Will was just 16 years old and had everything to prove, while Mitchell had arrived first-team ready.

Like Mitchell, Hastie had a UK passport through family connections with the country he would make his home for a while. His father also hailed from Glasgow, though his loyalties were with the club from Parkhead rather than Ibrox. While Will's dad had emigrated to the other side of the world, he had plenty of extended family to connect with when he moved to Glasgow.

Naturally, signing for Celtic was a huge source of pride for all the family. Will recalled, "There's a newspaper article that shows my father in Australia lying under his Mercedes Benz with Celtic number plates. I'm pretty certain he was more proud than I was. My family in Scotland were pretty amazed that a relative from Australia had come and signed for the club. They were overjoyed and became my surrogate family from that moment on."

One unforeseen challenge would be in finding a home for a 16-year-old who had only vague memories of being in Scotland on a visit as a young boy. In 1989, Scottish football's infrastructure did not really cater to young boys living far from their home countries.

"I had been to Scotland as a young kid, but this was the first trip that I could really remember," said Will. "Dad had taken us back to see his homeland when I was around eight or nine, but the 1989 experience was the first trip when I was more aware of what was going on.

"Celtic tried to fix me up with some accommodation, but I only lasted about a week in a little room in Baillieston, [a Glasgow suburb] not far from the stadium. That didn't really work out for me, so I stayed with my uncle until we could find an alternative. I lived with my Uncle Brian, my dad's youngest brother, for a good three months before I sorted out accommodation.

"The family in the place in Baillieston had the best intentions but just didn't understand what a young professional athlete might need, especially in terms of diet. You could only eat fried eggs so often.

"Celtic had never had an Australian kid come and sign, so for them it was all new. There wasn't really any special support for what my needs might be as a young player coming over from Australia. I just had to fit in like one of the Scottish players. So my family was very helpful in that respect. They helped me get over the homesickness as best they could and created a settled environment.

"Interestingly, I was the only foreigner on the ground staff, so I stuck out like a sore thumb. It was pretty challenging for the first six months because you're not necessarily welcomed with open arms in that kind of competitive environment. So it took a good six months to feel accepted by the playing group, but that's not uncommon whenever you join a new club."

For many of the foreign players who move to various clubs in their career, being at Celtic is just another job—a big club in a small league, where the huge fan base demands success. They may grow to appreciate the club's history and the passion of the supporters. However, Will Hastie, as Tommy Burns famously described himself, seemed to be "a supporter who got lucky".

"I was obsessed with the club because of my dad," said Will. "I had Paul McStay posters on my wall from the *Shoot* magazine. I would go out and get the *Shoot* magazine every week, and most of my favourite players were Celtic players.

"I remember my dad being the first one in our neighbourhood to get a VHS video recorder. His uncle and brothers would send out VHS tapes of Celtic games, usually a week or two behind. That was the only way we were able to watch them then. It was my dream to play for the club and for that to be realised as a 16-year-old was pretty special. I might even have been a bit too young, in hindsight."

It wasn't apparent in the summer of 1989, but Celtic were about to slide into one of the worst spells in their history—a period that almost saw them go into administration in 1994. Scottish football's top-tier title had been contested by Celtic, Aberdeen and Dundee United in the early to mid-1980s, but the arrival of Graeme Souness as player-manager and some big investments by Rangers from 1986 changed all of that. The Bhoys battled gamely for a few years but mismanagement and financial challenges saw them become also-rans in the early 1990s.

One infamous episode brought home how much the balance of power had shifted between Celtic and Rangers around this time, while also highlighting the intensity of the rivalry between the Glasgow clubs. It centred around Maurice 'Mo' Johnston—a boyhood Celtic fan who had played for his favourite team from 1984 to 1987 before moving to Nantes in France. In the summer of 1989, he shook hands on a return to Parkhead and was pictured in a Celtic shirt with Billy McNeill before having a change of heart after receiving a better offer from a club flexing its financial muscles.

The move had the added controversy of Johnston becoming only the second player to cross 'the Old Firm divide' since World War II—and the first Catholic to openly play for Rangers since World War I.

Hastie recalled, "The year I arrived, Maurice Johnston was bought by Rangers, and that was one of the most eye-opening things I have ever seen. He had, of course, apparently agreed to rejoin Celtic but then switched sides and went to Ibrox. There was a lot of tension in the air, and on Johnston's first visit to Celtic Park as a Rangers player, I was on the ground staff pitch-side.

"There was actually a bomb scare at the stadium on the Friday before the game, which, as a young kid who had only just arrived in Scotland, was pretty interesting. We were wearing shorts and T-shirts outside the ground for an extended period until they cleared the stadium. I remember standing there waiting and being absolutely freezing.

"It was the early phase of the Souness reign. Celtic had won their Centenary Double the previous year and beat Rangers in the Scottish Cup final in 1989, so the atmosphere was still pretty buoyant coming into the 1989–90 season, but that turned out to be the first of five consecutive trophyless seasons."

Coming to the club he had supported meant that Hastie had to be careful not to seem starstruck, but he had already met one particular hero over in Australia. When the Socceroos and Scotland met in the playoff for the 1986 World Cup finals, Paul McStay travelled to Melbourne for the second leg. For Hastie, this was too good an opportunity to miss.

"At the World Cup playoff second leg, I was 12 years of age. I said to my dad that he had to get me in to meet Paul McStay. I took my autograph book with me into the hotel lobby, and I still have a photo of me meeting Paul in 1985."

Meeting him again, in very different circumstances, four years later, McStay made a very positive impression for the way he interacted with Celtic's youth players.

"Paul McStay and Peter Grant were phenomenal," said Will. "Because Paul had come through the youth system, he spent a lot of time with the young players, trying to make them feel as welcome as possible.

"Paul and Peter stand out because they had come through the system, and they understood what it was about and what it felt like to be on the ground staff and to be in the youth team. They were heroes of mine. Paul Elliott had just joined the club from Pisa, and he had a different kind of aura about him—more international, more designer, more cool. He was someone that had a personality that drove things. Big Roy Aitken was still there and still very much a strong influence."

While several of the first-team squad made an impact on Hastie, the club's history was still well represented by some big names from the past.

"While he wasn't necessarily a hero of mine, Neily Mochan ran the ground staff," Will recalled. "My father thought very highly of him, so he was a connection to my dad. My dad's hero Bobby Lennox was on the coaching staff, and that reminded me of how I grew up getting a dollar if I could name the starting XI of Celtic's 1967 European champions. Jimmy Johnstone was another player who became familiar to us, and, of course, Billy McNeil was the gaffer."

While there was the glamour of being around some of the biggest names from present and past, there was not always glamour in being part of the youth setup in the days before pampering young players became more common.

"This was still in the era when we were designated 'a professional', and we had to clean their boots and look after their kits," said Will. "I remember cleaning about 60 pairs of boots a day for the better part of two years, which wasn't the most fun job. When I dreamt of becoming a professional football player, I didn't think I would be doing that."

While shining up the boots of the first-team squad was not a job that any youth team player particularly relished, there were still plenty of highlights during Hastie's two years at Celtic. The one that stands out was when he got the opportunity to lift some silverware wearing the green and white.

"We won the Glasgow Cup in my second year at the club, which was probably the highlight. It had become a tournament for reserve sides by that time. For me, it was the first trophy, it was at Parkhead, and there was a nice little crowd. To actually win a trophy at Parkhead wearing the green and white hoops was pretty special. I still have a team photo of that on my wall, and it's probably my favourite memory of my time there."

There is, sadly, a bittersweet aspect to that photo, as it serves as a reminder of the premature passing of a good friend.

"A youngster called Stuart Gray had come up from Leeds United to join the ground staff at that time," Will recalled. "Because we were the only two who were living far from our homes, we became really close, and in that photo, Stuart has his arm around me. Of course, Stuart passed away last year [2024, after a battle with cancer], which was really heartbreaking."

While that 3–2 victory over Partick Thistle in the Glasgow Cup final was a memorable moment, the end to Will's time at Parkhead soon followed. And, unfortunately, it was something that he didn't see coming.

"It was a real shock. I actually thought things were going well. All the feedback had been really positive. I was expecting to stay and had delayed my trip back to Australia until I could get a final decision on where I was going at the end of the 1990–91 season."

Hastie was so focused on staying in Glasgow and extending his contract with Celtic that he effectively made himself unavailable for selection for Australia's squad for the 1991 U20 World Cup: "Delaying the trip back prevented me from getting selected for the Australia U20 team that reached the semi-finals of the U20 World Cup in Portugal that year.

"Earlier in the year, I had actually been part of the team that qualified for the tournament. I ended up waiting too long in Scotland to see whether I would get another contract and missed out on the final selection for that Australia team as well. So I got hit by a double whammy in the space of two weeks by just hanging on in the hope of getting another deal."

On that fateful day when Billy McNeill and Tommy Craig broke the news that Hastie's future wasn't to be at Celtic, Hastie could not wait to get out of the city that he had hoped to make his home for the foreseeable future. Even the presence of a fellow Aussie at Dundee couldn't encourage him to make the trip to the east of Scotland that Celtic had offered.

"That was it. I had to pack my stuff up, and I wanted to get home as quickly as possible. I didn't particularly want to go to Dundee. A good mate of mine called Lachlan Armstrong was there, and I called him to tell him what had happened, but I just wanted to get home as soon as possible.

"Ironically, I ended up at Dundee about six months later, having trialled at Ipswich Town and Sunderland, which didn't work out for me. I stayed in Dundee for a year, but I didn't settle there. I just didn't feel like I was progressing with my football. Maybe it was just the culmination of three years of grind, of constantly trying to prove yourself from the age of 16 to 19. If you're not in a settled environment, that can be quite challenging. I didn't take to Dundee as a town anywhere near as much as I took to Glasgow."

With his time up in Scotland, the Celtic connection took him to a place in Ireland that he was not too familiar with. Paul McStay's older brother Willie, who had also played for Celtic, had been appointed player-manager at Sligo Rovers and felt that Hastie could do a job for his new club.

"Willie had left Celtic by the time I was there, and he was at Kilmarnock for a spell to finish his career," said Will. "I didn't make a connection with Willie while I was at Celtic, but I had been close to Paul and Willie's brother Raymond, who had played in the reserves with me. Willie called to say he had just taken the manager's job at Sligo Rovers, and he was putting together a young team. He asked if I would be interested in going over. I had never even heard of Sligo in my life. I went over on a one-month contract and ended up spending three really enjoyable years at Sligo.

"I then moved back to Australia and played for a team called Gippsland Falcons in the National Soccer League for roughly five seasons. That was really enjoyable. I was training four nights a week and on a plane every weekend for games around Australia. And I still had time to study.

"That probably wouldn't have ended but for the league collapsing. There was an 18-month hiatus between the NSL and the A-League. At that point, I was 30 and by the time the A-League got going, no one really wanted a 32-year-old box-to-box midfielder. I felt my career ended when the NSL ended."

Hastie's time at Celtic may have ended somewhat abruptly, and his career may not have reached the heights he had hoped for when he put pen to paper for his heroes. However, he remains one of the very few "supporters who got lucky". In addition to the football side of things, Hastie also got to make much stronger connections with the family members in Glasgow that were so distant when he was growing up.

"You've always got to look back on the positive experiences. It turned me from a boy into a man really quickly, and maybe it was quicker than it needed to be in terms of my football development. But it gave me the values, the skills and the learning that I still use in my life to this day as a 51-year-old. I'm very grateful for the experience and very grateful that I managed to achieve what was a lifelong dream as a 16-year-old.

"Not many people can say that they played for their boyhood club having grown up supporting them. I've nothing but happy memories of it. And I'm also thankful for how my cousins in Glasgow and the UK became like brothers and sisters instead of just cousins. I'm grateful that I got the opportunity to get to know them better, and they were the ones who took great care of me."

A career in what can obviously be quite a cutthroat business hardened Hastie, and he no longer has the same passion for the team he once idolised. However, the McStay connection keeps him tied to Celtic.

"I still keep in touch with Willie, who has a role at Parkhead," said Will. "In January 2022, I went back to Scotland for my 50th birthday to say a big thanks to my family over there for everything they have done for me. And I caught up with Willie and his wife Mary. Ironically, Paul works in Sydney now, so I catch up with Paul, and we have a coffee together about once every six months.

"On my first day at Celtic, they did a time trial for preseason training. Everyone went off at 10-second intervals, and I ran my hardest and chased down Paul and got to run alongside him for a while just because I wanted to say hi to him. They say never meet your heroes, but Paul was the loveliest guy you could meet and still is.

"I still watch the big Celtic games but I don't watch every week. It was a club that was the love of my life but fandom is a bit different from professional football. It was pretty brutal the way it ended, and I'm not an obsessed fan anymore. I did realise pretty quickly that you have to separate fandom from playing. I would go into the dressing room after an Old Firm game and be surprised that some of the players didn't seem as upset about a defeat to Rangers as my father would be. I think that's just the reality of a professional player."

Hastie was one of several Australian teenagers to try his luck in Scotland in the late 1980s and early 1990s. In addition to Lachlan Armstrong, Hastie recalled meeting one of them felt a bit like crossing into enemy territory.

"There was a young lad at Rangers at the time called Craig Lewis—I knew him from Victoria," Will recalled. "We used to hang out together, but it almost felt like a secret date with a mate because he was a Rangers player. He was another one who went through the youth system and didn't quite get a first-team appearance."

The end of Hastie's time at Celtic may have been unpleasant but the fact that he was there in the first place was further evidence that the reputation of Aussie players was on the rise.

Lachlan Armstrong

"Aw fuck, I was going to start you this weekend against Rangers."

Lachlan Armstrong wasn't sure if Dundee boss Jim Duffy was messing with his head or being genuine when he suggested the Australian was going to get the opportunity to play against the team that his dad and many of his extended family supported.

Armstrong said, "I'll never know if he was just saying that to try and get me to hang around longer. And it was against Rangers, of all clubs, given my family connection. But I look back and it does show just how much I wanted to move back to Australia. So I was released from my contract."

Lachlan Armstrong's time in Scotland did not end in the same heartbreaking circumstances as Will Hastie's had. He was a regular in Dundee's first-team squad and had made a couple of appearances for them. However, the lure of a return to the homeland proved stronger than the will to pursue a dream that had become more challenging since a serious knee injury interrupted his progress.

Lachlan's father, Jimmy, is Australian football royalty, though his upbringing was in Glasgow, and he didn't arrive in Australia until the age of 23. His record of 152 goals in the Victorian State League stood for almost 30 years. Jimmy has also been inducted into the Football Australia Hall of Fame. Best known for his time at South Melbourne Hellas in the 1970s, part of his Hall of Fame entry on the Football Australia website reads, "… he was instrumental in steering the club to three championships in that period, cementing himself as an all-time great of the club."

So Lachlan, like Dave Mitchell and Will Hastie, had a Scottish father. Jimmy Armstrong's name carried significant weight in Aussie football circles, and his background in Scottish junior football (semi-professional) at Renfrew and Yoker Athletic may have had an influence on Dundee's decision to take a chance on Lachlan.

Lachlan said, "I was 16 at the time, and I was travelling with a select team from Melbourne that was going to play in the Aberdeen International Football Festival. Then we were going to play in an international tournament in Aberystwyth that was, I think, sponsored by Ian Rush.

"It was a select team, and with Dad being a footballer and a Glaswegian, he wrote to a lot of clubs to tell them that I was coming over and asked if they wouldn't mind sending some scouts to have a look at me. That's how the move to Dundee came about.

"I think one of the things that opened the door—and I still have a copy of it at home—was the letter that Dad wrote to clubs, and it mentioned that he had been a former junior footballer in Glasgow and had gone on to represent Australia when he became a citizen.

"So I think that letter highlighted the fact that there was some pedigree there and I was worth a look. I'm sure clubs received lots of letters, but they actually took this one half-seriously—at least Dundee did.

"I ended up playing really well in both tournaments, and the first point of contact after the Aberdeen tournament was a scout from Dundee called Bert Slater. He was the goalkeeper coach at Dundee at the time. So Dundee were the first club to reach out after the tournament and they offered me a trial.

"First I went to play in the Aberystwyth tournament and then went back to Dundee for the trial. This was the summer of 1989."

Like Will Hastie, it was a huge gamble for a 16-year-old to settle on the other side of the world despite having the support of extended family. And Armstrong knows that, if it hadn't been for the tragic passing of his mother a year earlier, he might not have been allowed to take that gamble at such a young age.

"I lost my mum when I was 15—a year before. Mum was a high school vice-principal, and I'm sure if she had been around, she would have said there was no way I was going to pursue my dream without having an academic option as well.

"But Dad was left with me and my brother, and he said 'if you want to follow your dreams, go and do it'. From a football perspective back then, it was just me wanting to become a professional footballer. And dad was totally happy for me— he comes from a big family, and I had aunts and uncles, not just in Glasgow but all over Britain. They were all delighted for me to be having my first chance and live the dream.

"I had an uncle in Baillieston, so I based myself in Glasgow. Back then, players on the YTS (Youth Training Scheme) didn't play for the club on the weekend as they were too young to play reserve-team football. So they went back to their home regions and played local football at weekends. And we all got together on a Monday on the train and headed back to Dundee for the week, where we stayed in digs."

At a time when Scottish football still consisted mainly of Scottish players, like Will Hastie, Armstrong stood out among the other YTS boys.

"For the local lads, it was unique to have someone from the other side of the world there," said Lachlan. "It was a mixture of lads from across Scotland. There were some local Dundonians and a batch from the rest of the country. I tagged along with the Glasgow batch. But every week, they would be coming from Edinburgh and Fife and all over."

Despite his youth and being thrust into an unfamiliar environment, Armstrong soon found his feet. Coming from elsewhere turned out to be something that helped rather than hindered him at times.

"The accent opened lots of doors," he recalled. "You started chatting to somebody and they wanted to know where you were from and what you were doing in Scotland. When you told them you were a footballer, it made it even more interesting in such a passionate football culture. At the time, there weren't that many Aussies around, so it was a bit of a rarity to be an Australian out there. In that regard, it meant people were more welcoming and wanted to have a chat about my story."

Off the field, fitting in was relatively straightforward, but the style of football required a period of adaptation. Lachlan added, "The football culture was spiky and intense in training and it took a little bit of getting used to. But I was loving every minute of it, training every day."

In addition to the daily training sessions, there was a requirement to continue his schooling at a local further education college. However, it seemed more like a box-ticking exercise that was not treated with any great respect by the young players, whose focus was solely on football.

"A day and a half a week, the YTS boys went to college but I don't think we took that as seriously as my late mum would have wanted," said Lachlan. "Classes were almost all sports related. But one day they sent us for some training in work as receptionists—they had us answering phones, which was a bit weird.

"Mostly, it was learning about how to coach the basics of different kinds of sports. You can imagine with 15 young footballers going to college, we walk in with our Dundee gear... It was a bit of a piss-take to be honest."

Armstrong's links to his new home did help, but he had known very little about his new club before joining them. And in the season that he arrived, the first team would be relegated from the Premier League to the First Division for the first time in 14 years, while his dad's favourite side lifted their second successive top-tier title.

"Dad was a big Rangers fan, and his family were all Rangers fans," Lachlan recalled. "It was not like we ever got to watch it, but *Shoot* magazine was everyone's weekly, and there were a few pages on Scottish football there. When I got to Scotland, my uncle took me to watch Rangers in preseason friendlies."

It would have surprised the younger Lachlan (as it does most non-Dundee fans to this day) to learn that, 26 years earlier, his new club had beaten Koln, Sporting Lisbon and Anderlecht on their way to the European Cup semi-final, where they were beaten by eventual winners AC Milan. When Dundee United reached the same stage of the competition in 1984, it meant that Dundee was one of a select few cities to have had two clubs feature at that stage of the tournament. In 2024, the number still stood at just seven, Glasgow being one of the others.

Lachlan admitted, "Going over to Scotland, I didn't know much about Dundee at all, other than having an awareness from looking at the league tables in *Shoot*. That was a lot of people's understanding of UK football in Australia at the time. I knew of the Scottish Premier League, but mostly focusing on Rangers."

While the schedule of games, training and college visits kept Armstrong busy enough, he still valued the opportunities to catch up with a friend from his home country. Will Hastie's support acted as a vital bridge between his new life in Scotland and the country of his childhood.

"Will and I caught up with each other at weekends when I went back to Glasgow," Lachlan recalled. "Will would either come over to my uncle's place, or I'd go over to his digs, and we'd just hang out together and share our experiences. I think if we hadn't had each other, the experience might have been more short-lived."

Armstrong and Hastie weren't the only people at the club who were far from home. Canadian businessman Ron Dixon took over Dundee in 1992 and, following the club's promotion to the Premier League, his offer of a reward did not go down too well.

"I remember the discontent in the dressing room because Ron Dixon didn't want to give the players a cash bonus," said Lachlan. "He wanted to give them a ring, a typical American and Canadian thing.

"The players were like, 'fuck that, who wants a ring? Give us the cash bonus or send us on an end-of-season trip to Ibiza or somewhere like that'. The players weren't interested in getting a ring. I remember that vividly."

It was on a visit home that Armstrong's steady progress towards the Dundee first team seemed to have ended very abruptly. What looked like a good opportunity to develop some experience in senior football almost put an end to his time on Tayside. Things were really looking good at the end of the 1991–92 season, with Armstrong shining in the Dundee reserve team and the first team winning promotion. But a holiday back in Australia resulted in the 19-year-old taking an unwanted extended break.

"I had a really good season when I was top scorer for the reserves and the senior team got promoted to the Premier League," Lachlan recalled. "I went back to Australia and got a phone call, randomly, from one of the local clubs—Sunshine George Cross. They asked if I would be interested in playing a few games on loan. I jumped at the chance because I hadn't played any senior football until that point, albeit that it would be at a much lower level than the Scottish First Division or Premier League.

"Sunshine George Cross were a National League team that had just been relegated to the state league. Back then, there was a summer national league and a winter premier league. I signed up for four to six games in the winter league.

"One of the things that prevented me from making my debut was that there had to be an insurance policy, and I had to go to Lloyd's Bank or somewhere to get that policy. I also had to do the paperwork for an international transfer.

"So I agreed to play these games while I was on holiday in Australia, and in the third game, I busted my knee up. It was one of those decisions you look back on and think, 'I should have just enjoyed my holiday'.

"I copped a bad one in a 50-50 tackle, and I had to have a knee reconstruction. I stayed in Australia for my rehab, and that was probably one of the reasons I ended up seeing what I was missing. I had left Australia as a 16-year-old and had been away for three and a half years. I had only ever come back for three to four weeks in the middle of winter.

"All of a sudden, I was there in Australia, with my friends, seeing what Australian life was like for a 19-year-old. Nevertheless, I still got myself back to playing football, and I returned to Dundee after Christmas, worked myself back into the first team, got a new contract and played in the last game of that season."

But that return to Dundee came in rather bizarre circumstances. His failure to show up for preseason training triggered his dismissal despite the club being aware of his situation. Armstrong remains unsure if it was an administrative error based on HR procedures or if it was initiated by the club's management.

"Just after I had my knee reconstruction, I got a P45 in the mail," Lachlan recalled. "I remember getting that and thinking 'this is horrible'. There I was, wondering if I would ever play football again and receiving a P45. When they took me off the books, I was only getting about £40 a week or something crazy like that.

"It was a bit bittersweet going back there after I was fit. The club had cut me off, and six months later, I was back trying to prove myself, which I managed to do.

"Things had gone a bit weird at the club, and when I returned, there was a dog track around the pitch instead of the old ash track where I had thrown up many a time. Some really interesting changes had taken place. Every couple of weeks, it seemed a new foreigner would come into the dressing room."

The new foreign players meant increased competition, and Armstrong's first-team experience had been limited to friendlies. But at the end of the 1992–93 season, the trauma of the previous year would be forgotten when he finally made his debut.

"Just being there playing youth football and reserve football was living the dream," said Lachlan. "In Dundee, you would go to the boot room before games because that's where they hung up the squads on the wall.

"When you see your name in the first-team squad as a young man from Australia, who had made so many sacrifices to be there, it was one of those moments that makes everything you have done worthwhile. Even if it was a friendly game or a preseason match, you feel that you've made it, even though you haven't really.

"The first games I played with the first team were pre-season friendlies against Celtic and Wimbledon, who had John Fashanu at the time. I distinctly remember their style of play—put it in the mixer.

"When I went there and was on trial as a 16-year-old, I had this ridiculous rich vein of form. I remember I had a scrap book and I would write down all my games. So, there were youth games, and I would score a few goals. And then there were reserve games. I remember being taken to Falkirk one Wednesday night. It was a mixture of first team and reserves, and I had been taken to carry the hampers and enjoy the experience.

"I didn't think anything of it at the time, but someone told me that I had been doing so well that they wanted to give me the opportunity to see things at the next level. That was a crazy three or four months when I hit the ground running as a 16-year-old, but I didn't really get into the first-team squad on a regular basis until the promotion year of 1991–92. But I never actually got on the pitch or made it into the matchday squad. I was always watching from the stands."

On a historic occasion in May 1993, Armstrong would not be watching from the stands. He would be playing in front of the Jungle—the fabled terraced enclosure at Celtic Park.

As Celtic's European Cup winning captain Billy McNeill once put it: "The Jungle made a major contribution to success at Celtic Park before, during and after my days there. The volume of support and the understanding of knowledge shown by the fans there is legendary."

The Jungle was so famous that John Quinn wrote a book about it. *Jungle Tales: Celtic Memories of an Epic Stand* features the above quote and highlights the Jungle's place in Celtic's history.

"When it came to my turn to run out and face the Jungle for the first time I found it a truly incredible experience … it was an awesome sight and sound," said Tommy Burns, his words a measure of the impact this special part of the stadium had on the players.

But Lachlan Armstrong's competitive first-team debut would coincide with the Jungle's last stand. The United Kingdom government's Taylor Report dictated that all stadiums would have to be all-seated, leading to the demise of Celtic's much-loved Jungle.

"My first competitive appearance was at Celtic Park in the last-ever game of the Jungle," Lachlan recalled. "That came at the end of the season when I made my comeback from knee reconstruction, and I think I only landed back in Scotland in January of that year. I worked really hard to get myself back to match fitness, and was doing well in the reserves.

"It was the last game of the season, and we were safe from relegation. I think I lasted maybe an hour or something like that. It was pretty surreal.

"It's strange explaining to people now that during my time in Scotland, it was very much Rangers and Aberdeen competing for the title, and people find it hard to fathom where Celtic were at back then. I tell people I made my debut against the third-best team in Scotland. For us it was a dead rubber, which probably led to me getting a start."

The significance of the occasion was somewhat lost on Armstrong. He had no real awareness of the Jungle's place in Scottish football culture. The only thing that mattered to him was his performance.

"I put pressure on myself," he said. "I was absolutely shitting myself walking out and warming up. But, as is typically the case, the game gets underway, and you get on with it. Jim Duffy—our playing assistant manager—missed a penalty in the first half that would have put us 1-0 up. Typically, for one of the bottom sides against one of the top sides, we didn't have a lot of the ball, and I didn't get a lot of touches. But I remember being happy with my performance. I would have liked to have stayed on for a lot longer, but I remember it being a good day, though a nerve-wracking one in the lead-up."

While making a solid debut might sometimes act as a springboard to success, not much changed after that match. Armstrong would make just one more first-team appearance in a competitive match, coming on as a second-half substitute in a 2-0 league defeat at Hibs in August 1993.

The end of Armstrong's time at Dundee was approaching, but it had been quite the journey.

"In my third year there, I was top scorer for the reserve team," said Lachlan. "I loved scoring goals, so other than the time when I was in and around the first team, that was definitely a highlight. The debut against Celtic is certainly the high point."

Armstrong had also played with some players who had achieved a lot, and others who would go on to have excellent careers for club and country.

"Neil McCann was a couple of years younger than me. I remember him coming through as a real cocky type," Lachlan recalled. "Youngsters were all fighting hard to come through from the youth team to the first team. And I just remember him being cocky but also being a great player.

"I also remember Billy Dodds, who was a mainstay at the club and the main goal scorer in the time that I was there. He was someone that I, as a young striker, looked up to. He was quite good with the young lads."

McCann and Dodds would go on to star for Rangers alongside Craig Moore and Tony Vidmar, while also winning multiple caps for Scotland. While this pair were stars of the future, Armstrong felt pity for a Scotland and Aberdeen great who had ended up at Dundee after being ruthlessly demoted by Alex Ferguson at Manchester United.

"When Jim Leighton joined, he was in horrible form," said Lachlan. "It was sad to see the form he was in. I remember him being sent to train with us, the young players, in the afternoon. He had served his nation proudly, and there he was in the afternoon with the young lads, working his arse off, but with the youngsters taking the piss a little bit."

It wasn't always easy being a youth or reserve team player. It could make you a target for the older players as the hierarchy of the time dictated. But future Adelaide Force midfielder Derek Ferguson, who joined Dundee on a loan spell from Rangers, wasn't having any of it.

"I distinctly remember when Derek Ferguson came on loan," said Lachlan. "I wouldn't say it was extreme bullying but there was a lot of shit that went down between senior players, and they'd treat the young players like absolute shit.

"I remember Derek actually standing up to the senior players and saying, 'don't treat these kids like that'. That's a memory that I take away because it didn't happen too often. It was always like, 'let's get stuck into the young kids'. There was always a fear factor, and the kids didn't want to make a mistake because the senior pros would come down hard on them."

More than three decades on, much has changed in Scottish football culture. It still seems slightly shocking how things were in the early 90s.

"I remember when I was 18–19, and you played, and then you would go out, but not just for a couple of beers," Lachlan recalled. "You would go out and you would get absolutely smashed. You would recover the next day or sometimes you were in for training the next morning and you would just sweat it out, work hard and work through it.

"I think it was the culture of the country at the time. I don't know about now—but it certainly was then. There was no 'let's look after our bodies, we're professional footballers'. It was play hard and party hard, and then sweat it out.

"One thing I still laugh about is that I stayed in digs for the first few years, and the pre-match meal was always a fry-up. Imagine trying to say that to the kids these days. You had Scottish square sausage, black pudding, beans and eggs as your pre-match meal. You had to carry that around with you on the field. The professionalism was not what it is in the modern day.

"I remember on my 20th birthday we had an evening reserve game against Rangers that was postponed, and everyone was buzzing because it meant we could go out. The whole squad agreed to go out for my birthday, and we got totally smashed. The next day there was a game that we weren't supposed to be involved in because we had been in the squad for the Rangers game.

"But the teams went up, and we were all hungover. And I just remember us all seeing our names on this list and thinking, 'Jesus Christ, we've got to go and play tonight.'.

"I look back at it now and think of it as a very Scottish thing. They go out and party and then they come to work and they work their arses off."

Another aspect of playing at a Scottish club was the focus given to cardio and developing the ability to run at an intense level for 90 minutes.

"In training, we sometimes had these things called track sessions when you wouldn't even see a ball. You'd sometimes get to training, and it was horrible to hear the coach come in and say, 'Right lads, we're on the track'.

"Sometimes, we'd train first and then get on the track. As a reserve team, we'd often have Saturday and Sunday off and play Monday night. The penalty for having the weekend off was that they absolutely killed you on Friday.

"The track sessions were some of the most gruelling things I've ever done in my life. Lots of people would be throwing up, and sometimes I think that was the coaches' aim.

"Now I am a coach, I can't remember a lot of real technical sessions. I remember it being just gung-ho, work hard, get stuck in—very much the football of the day. When I transitioned back to Australia, people there were shocked by the work ethic I had. Scottish football was just helter-skelter, run until you drop."

Things were beginning to change as the number of foreign players increased dramatically towards the middle of the 1990s. However, Dundee did not select the wisest accommodation for some of their newest recruits from overseas.

"At the end of my time at Dundee, around 1993, when I decided it was time to go home, there were so many foreigners at Dundee," Lachlan recalled. "There must have been around 12 to 14. The majority lived at this pub in Broughty Ferry called The Fort. I think one of the directors at the club owned the Fort Bar and it had rooms above it. It just perpetuated the culture. All these people lived above a bar, while I lived across the road in a flat."

Five years later, Morten Wieghorst would be a Scottish Premier League champion with Celtic—and he would play for Denmark in the 1998 World Cup finals, over two decades before he would be appointed as manager of his national team. Among his formative football experiences was sharing a flat near the Fort Bar, and looking a little out of place.

"I lived with Morten Wieghorst for a couple of months," said Lachlan.

"He was a young Dane and he was super professional. All the players who came from other European countries were a little bit different, so the British culture was an eye opener for them.

"I remember Morten had these really colourful jumpers and Mickey Mouse patches on his denims and thinking, woah, my new roommate's a bit weird."

While Wieghorst didn't quite fit into the drinking culture of the day, a more experienced Scottish player was immersed in it.

"Ian McCall was another one who stood out," Lachlan recalled. "He was a different kind of Scotsman, or at least he saw himself as different. I think he came through university. Will and I had a couple of wild nights with Ian.

"I remember when we were living in Broughty Ferry and we got kicked out of the lounge bar because Ian was swearing. Me and Will were only 19 at the time, but as we were leaving, Ian passed his glass to the barman, but then wouldn't let go of it. They were in a bit of a standoff and eyeballing each other. And then Ian just said, 'Fuck, fuck, bastard, cunt!'—and then walked out! He was a bit crazy."

Though Armstrong was having fun on occasion, and managed to stay in the first-team squad, he couldn't shake those memories of an extended stay in Australia that reminded him of what an alternative lifestyle could be.

"I was looking back, remembering that I really enjoyed my time at home. I was genuinely homesick," he recalled.

And then came that decision to reveal his plan to return home to Jim Duffy, only to hear the 'revelation' that he was in the gaffer's plans for a match against Rangers.

Instead of Dundee versus Rangers, it was time for Armstrong's National League career to get going.

As for Dundee, they would have to wait a few years before they had a Socceroo who would make a bigger impact. Chris Coyne arrived at Dens Park in 2000. He was followed by Mark Robertson a year later. It was an interesting time to be at the club, with the likes of Claudio Caniggia and Temuri Ketsbaia among a cast of international stars.

The best part of a decade before that, Lachlan Armstrong had decided to give up on Dundee and head home to Victoria.

"Morwell Falcons was the team I returned to play for," he recalled. "They had a Scottish manager called Bobby McClachlan. I had a couple of seasons there, and then I had a spell in Malaysia with Melaka. I played against Brunei and scored a hattrick when Mick Lyons, the Everton legend, was the coach there.

"Lyons was about to get a job in Australia with a new franchise club called Canberra Cosmos. I had a ripper game, and Mick asked me if I wanted to go back to Australia with him. I had a couple of years in Canberra but I wasn't really making any money out of football, and I guess it was time to look for a real job.

"That realisation coincided with me finding out that my knee was in pretty bad shape anyway. So I started playing local football, got a day job and had a normal life outside football. I was about 25–26 when I made the decision to go back to part-time football. For the whole time I was a professional footballer, I was living pay cheque to pay cheque.

"I guess I'm fortunate that I saw things from a realistic perspective, but I always kept my hand in by playing at a lower level and, when I stopped playing, getting involved in coaching."

That coaching saw him work with former Rangers left-back Stuart Munro at Melbourne Knights. Lachlan said, "That was a big thing for me because obviously I knew Stuart as a Rangers legend. Just having him around and learning from him was really great."

As of 2024, Armstrong continues to work in football, helping youngsters in Singapore prepare for overseas scholarships. And he continues to refer back to his experiences in the east of Scotland over 30 years later.

"Dad was a footballer and I had a good upbringing as a young footballer in Australia," said Lachlan. "But the footballer and person that I turned out to be was very much made in Dundee over those four years. I owe everything I did in football to those four years. It was an amazing time.

"In Singapore now, we're sending a lot of kids overseas on scholarships. I tell these kids how lucky they are with technology because back in those days, Will and I were calling home on reverse charges, writing letters and making video cassettes where we would talk into the camera and send them home. It's so much easier for kids nowadays to move to the other side of the world. We had some tough times where we missed our family and friends. It isn't the same for kids these days."

The stories of Will Hastie, Lachlan Armstrong and Craig Lewis have similarities, while Scott Playle and Alistair Edwards were two more young Aussies who could not establish themselves at Ibrox. But it wouldn't be long before Craig Moore became the first Socceroo in Scotland to make a sustained impact.

CHAPTER 3
The Breakthrough Star

In an interview in German magazine *11 Freunde*, the legendary Celtic and Sweden striker Henrik Larsson revealed his toughest opponent: "It was Craig Moore of Rangers. He yelled at me for 90 minutes, kicked me across the pitch and tried everything to get inside my head.

"But you have to give him one thing, he never complained when he got something back himself. And I got him back really hard a few times!"

Speaking on *Go Radio*, Moore said in response, "When you hear those kinds of comments from such a fantastic player like Henrik Larsson, you have a little smile. It's nice to be respected, I guess, for what you've done as a footballer. We enjoyed some fantastic tussles."

A decade after Dave Mitchell made the move from Australia to Glasgow, following in his footsteps was 18-year-old defender Craig Moore—a student at the Australian Institute of Sport. Moore impressed at the 1993 World Youth Cup, which was held in his homeland, and captured the attention of two of the biggest clubs in Great Britain.

Opting for one club over another after a successful trial as an 18-year-old may not exactly have been a sliding doors moment, but if he had chosen differently, the young defender may have found himself battling for a place in the team against Tony Adams, Martin Keown and Steve Bould at Arsenal. Breaking into the Gunners' formidable defensive unit of the 1990s would certainly have been a challenge. As it was, Moore's "gut feeling" saw him choose Glasgow over London, but he would nonetheless find himself playing alongside some world-class talent, perhaps sooner than expected.

Unlike Dave Mitchell's difficult journey to his dream destination, there would be no contractual difficulties to resolve and plane journeys on someone else's ticket. Moore flew across the world hoping to secure a deal that would set up a successful career in the game. Until that point, more than any club in Scotland, Rangers had shown an interest in bringing in players from Australia, so it was clear that they had confidence that one of these moves would eventually work out.

In an interview with *SBS Sport*, Moore described how he got his big opportunity at Rangers.

"It came on the back of the 1993 World Youth Cup in Australia. After the tournament, I was approached by a couple of agents for trials with Arsenal and Rangers. I got offers from both clubs, and I eventually chose Rangers, purely on instinct and gut feeling, even though I knew very little about Scottish football. I guess I made the right decision because I kind of did well there."

He did indeed do well, lifting six Scottish Premier League titles, three Scottish Cups and three League Cups. Moore's 12 winning medal haul in Glasgow puts him pretty high on the list of Rangers Most Decorated Players of All Time. For perspective, he is just three trophies off Barry Ferguson's 15, which places the midfielder at No. 9 on the list. And Moore is just four behind John Greig, the man who brought Dave Mitchell to Ibrox and a player widely regarded as the greatest Ger in the club's history.

Like Greig, Moore broke into the Rangers first-team squad as a teenager, and most fans were surprised to see the name of this 18-year-old Aussie in the starting XI for the match against Dundee United on April 5th, 1994. This was a Rangers side that featured Andy Goram and Richard Gough, two of the finest players in the club's history, while Dave McPherson (who we'll talk more about later) was also in the defence alongside Moore. Up front for Rangers was Duncan Ferguson, a player who failed to make an impact for the Ibrox men but who would, of course, become an iconic figure at Everton.

In terms of the quality of the game at Tannadice, it wasn't the most memorable start in Scottish football. However, Moore did make a very positive impression on one watching football reporter.

Alex Cameron of *The Scottish Daily Record* wrote a fairly scathing introduction to his match report: "Rangers won't want to be reminded of Tannadice last night when the season's roll of honour is laid out. In truth, it was a fairly miserable contest..."

However, Cameron would go on to highlight the role played by a certain young Australian.

"The big shock before kick-off was the inclusion of young Craig Moore in the

Rangers line-up. Moore, 18, has been six months at Ibrox, having preferred joining Rangers to Arsenal. He was schooled in Australian football, and on last night's showing at right-back, he is a star in the making."

High praise indeed from the veteran journalist, whose words would prove wise in the years ahead.

Injuries to Gary Stevens and John Brown had given Moore his big chance, and he could obviously be satisfied to make a debut that featured a clean sheet. However, the Gers still had a league title to seal and a Scottish Cup to fight for, and Moore would make no more appearances that season. Instead, he would make his real breakthrough in 1994–95.

Stevens, Oleh Kuznetsov, Steven Pressley and Dave McPherson all left Ibrox between July and October 1994, potentially clearing the path for Moore to slot in at right-back or central defence.

However, in came Scotland international Alan McLaren, another player who could play right-back or centre-back; Alec Cleland, a right-back; and, most eye-catching of all, Basile Boli, the central defender who had scored the winning goal in the Champions League final just over a year beforehand.

Moore would comfortably outshine all three in terms of his contribution to the club in the years to come, albeit largely down to injuries in the case of McLaren. Boli, despite his status as a Champions League winner and a France international, failed to consistently impress for Rangers and lasted just a year, while Moore quietly started to establish himself, even though there was further competition in the shape of club stalwarts Gough and Brown.

The 1994–95 season would again see Rangers finish as the top team in the country, but it wasn't all smooth sailing. Moore was not involved when the Gers crashed out of the Champions League in the first round, losing home and away to AEK Athens. This was a huge disappointment for a club that had invested a lot in building a squad capable of making an impact at the highest level, the team having come close to reaching the final just 18 months earlier.

Just three days after the home defeat to AEK, Moore had his first taste of the Old Firm derby in August. Unfortunately for him, he was watching from the bench, and, unfortunately for Rangers, they surprisingly lost 2–0 to Celtic.

After the derby defeat, a hysterical piece in *The Sun* by Graham Clark suggested that Rangers "could be 90 minutes from complete disaster". A more sober observation was the criticism of a lineup that effectively meant that four centre-backs started against Celtic, with Dave McPherson and Steven Pressley pressed into service at full-back. With right-back Gary Stevens out injured, Clark added, "... this must be the time to give young Craig Moore a run".

Manager Walter Smith may or may not have read that article, but he did start Moore in that week's League Cup Third Round match at home to Falkirk. Things got worse for Rangers and Moore before they got better—they lost 2-1 to continue a miserable start to the campaign.

After that, Moore did get more game time, starting in a 3-0 home win against Hearts 10 days later, and then again as the Gers took revenge with a 2-0 league win at Falkirk the following weekend. A week later, there was another landmark as Moore netted his first Rangers goal in a 2-2 draw at Aberdeen.

Moore started the next four league matches, two of which ended in defeat, and found himself out in the cold for what would be a huge turning point in the season.

Alan McLaren had signed from Hearts for a significant fee that month, and he would make his debut against Celtic in October. The Bhoys' promising start to the season had fizzled out, but Rangers had experienced their own problems, so they were determined to earn the victory that would effectively end Celtic's bid to be among the challengers for their title. One big difference between this match and the one two months earlier was the form of Brian Laudrup. In August, Laudrup cut a forlorn figure at Ibrox as Celtic won 2-0. This time, he was the star of the show and almost single-handedly destroyed Celtic in a 3-1 victory.

Back in the starting lineup just a couple of weeks later, Moore then found himself on the bench again as the year drew to a close. It should be remembered that in December 1994, he turned 19.

Moore again missed out on a game against Celtic when the rivals drew 1-1 at Ibrox in January, meaning there would be just one more opportunity to get his first taste of the Old Firm derby that season.

In May 1995, Rangers had already clinched the Scottish Premier League title when they travelled to Hampden for their final encounter with Celtic that season. The Bhoys had a Scottish Cup final to look forward to a couple of weeks later, but they had little to play for but pride.

Moore relished the opportunity to finally play in the fixture but things did not exactly go as he'd hoped.

Moore recalled the match in an interview with *SBS*, saying, "Until you actually play in an Old Firm derby, you cannot appreciate what it really means to the fans of both sides. My first derby is a story in itself. It was a league match played at Hampden because Parkhead was being redeveloped. I scored an own goal and we got beat 3-0 by our biggest rivals. I had a good game but nobody remembers that. I tell you, that was a character-building experience for me. It taught me that you've got to fight for everything in football because nobody will do you any favours."

Moore was able to be philosophical about finding the wrong net in a match that did not count towards any prizes. The defender could also console himself with a league winner's medal in his first season as a core member of the first-team squad. Moreover, he'd become the first Aussie to become a Scottish Premier League champion—and he was still a teenager.

Rangers geared up for a new season and the opportunity to land an eighth title in succession, edging them closer to Celtic's coveted record of nine-on-the-spin.

Again, Walter Smith spent big on a player who would provide competition for Moore, Stephen Wright joining from Aberdeen as a right-back. Another player potentially standing in Moore's way was centre-back Gordan Petric, who moved to Ibrox from Dundee United. But the most notable addition to the squad in the summer of 1995 was Paul Gascoigne, a player who would ultimately prove the difference in a much tighter title race.

The start of that season must have left Moore to conclude that he was still seen as a squad player rather than a starter, with Wright understandably being the preferred option at right-back in the early stages of the season. It wasn't until mid-September that he made a league appearance, but Moore was out of favour again as Rangers won the first Old Firm match of the campaign, a 2-0 victory at Celtic Park.

With Rangers competing in the group stages of the Champions League, Moore was generally used as a rotation option, but he did finally get a shot at the big time when he was named in the starting lineup to face Juventus in Turin. However, Rangers were without their two biggest stars in Gascoigne and Laudrup. They suffered a 4-1 defeat, with Fabrizio Ravanelli (2), Antonio Conte and Alessandro Del Piero striking for the hosts.

It might have been a difficult night for Rangers, but it was another huge step in Moore's career, playing against the side that would become European champions that season, still a month shy of his 20th birthday.

Moore did not feature in the side that suffered an even heavier defeat in the return fixture as Juventus ran out 4-0 winners at Ibrox. Nor did he play in the team that drew 3-3 at home to Celtic in what was the match of the season and announced their bitter rivals as a force to be reckoned with for the first time in many years.

Celtic would push Rangers all the way in the title race, and, ultimately, the most important match of the league season would also turn out to be Moore's last of the campaign.

With Celtic just three points behind the league leaders on March 17th, the Glasgow rivals squared off for the final time in the 1995-96 league. A win for Rangers at Ibrox would have all but ensured their eighth successive title, but a late equaliser secured a 1-1 draw for Celtic and meant that there was still work to be done.

Unfortunately for Moore, he would take no further part in the battle for the league and Scottish Cup. The Australian suffered a foot injury in the first half of the match, keeping him out for the remainder of the season. He had to watch from the sidelines as his teammates lifted a league and cup double.

Even so, Moore's legacy was building. Another league title was in the bag, and another was to follow in 1996-97, when Rangers saw off a decent Celtic challenge once more. Recruitment in the summer of 1996 had brought in another competitor for a place in the backline, Sweden international Joachim Bjorklund arriving from Vicenza. Moore missed the first six weeks of the season through injury, but on his return, he would again feature regularly in a triumphant campaign. Of particular significance was the clinching of the ninth title in a row, matching the record that Celtic had set between 1966 and 1975.

There was now a huge incentive for Moore and his teammates to make further history by breaking the record. Rangers spent big again to try and secure an unprecedented 10 in a row. Moore's place in the side was to come under threat once more with the arrival of Lorenzo Amoruso, Stale Stensaas and right-back Sergio Porrini, who had been in the Juventus squad for their Champions League win just over a year beforehand. Compatriot Tony Vidmar was another recruit in the summer of 1997, along with Sweden international Jonas Thern and future Italy and AC Milan star Rino Gattuso.

If Rangers looked well set for their 10th title in a row, their main rivals appeared to be in disarray. Celtic lost the striking gifts of Pierre Van Hooijdonk, Paolo Di Canio and Jorge Cadete, though brought in a talented Swede called Henrik Larsson.

Moore started the first league match of the season, but the increased competition for places meant fewer starts during a campaign that ended in disappointment. There was something of an end-of-an-era feel, with Walter Smith announcing that this would be his final season as early as October 1997. Several players were in the twilight of their playing careers, and reaching the 10-in-a-row milestone would prove one step too far.

Celtic, revitalised by the management of Wim Jansen and the recruitment of the likes of Paul Lambert and Craig Burley, in addition to the outstanding Larsson, won the title on the final day. A week later, a defeat to Hearts in the Scottish Cup final meant that, for the first time since 1985–86, Rangers had a trophy-less season. Moore was on the bench for that final and stayed there.

The arrival of Dick Advocaat as manager saw big changes, but Moore seemed to be part of the Dutchman's plans as he made regular starts at the beginning of the 1998–99 season. But when Moore's former international team boss Terry Venables made a bid for the defender that autumn, he headed to London to join Crystal Palace.

After five largely successful years in Glasgow, Moore felt it was time for a new challenge—and Rangers, with a bloated squad, felt they could do without a player who, for all his qualities as a defensive utility player, had never quite become what could be described as a nailed-on starter. In an interview for the Rangers Museum website, Moore admitted as much, saying, "Although I was involved, I wasn't a starting XI player, and it took me the best part of six years to achieve that."

While this seemed like the end, Palace's misfortune turned out to be a lucky break for Rangers. Less than six months after he joined them on a four-year deal, the London club had to return Moore to his former club—financial problems meant that they failed to make the necessary payments before entering administration.

Still just 24 years old, Moore returned to Rangers ready to fight for a place in a team that had resumed its domestic dominance and won the league and Scottish Cup double in 1999. That long battle to be considered a starting player was finally won as Advocaat recognised Moore's qualities as a centre-back and trusted him throughout another successful season.

In his interview with the Rangers Museum website, Moore acknowledged the challenges he faced when he returned to Rangers and the need to earn Advocaat's approval.

"I really enjoyed it when I came back the second time around after a spell at

Crystal Palace," said Moore. "I know it doesn't always work out when you return somewhere, but I enjoyed a really successful time.

"Dick played me as a central defender, and I had to earn his trust— I remember he substituted me in one game after 23 minutes, so he wasn't all love, but I think once I came through that spell, I built trust with him and went on to play the best football of my career."

Rangers would win a second consecutive double in 1999-2000, with Moore heavily involved as Rangers impressed both at home and abroad. It is a season that stands out for Moore. He told SBS, "For me the finest Rangers team I played with was the one managed by Dick Advocaat in 1999-2000. We had won the league the season before and played in the UEFA Champions League against Bayern Munich, Valencia and PSV after beating Parma in the final qualifying round. That was an unbelievable team, and I'm proud to say I was a regular in defence."

The arrival of Martin O'Neill as Celtic manager in 2000 meant that competition between the Glasgow sides became fierce. The Bhoys would lift the next two league titles before another standout year for Moore in 2002-03. Compatriot Tony Vidmar left Rangers at the start of that season, but another Socceroo joined and together they won a treble.

Moore told the Rangers Museum website, "2002-03 was also a really satisfying year. I had struggled with injuries before that, but that particular season was a really good run of games. I also had my best mate in football, Kevin Muscat, over with me that year. Winning those trophies was fantastic but it was the way we went about it. We had a really good blend, there was so much talent and we really enjoyed ourselves."

Moore's early days at Ibrox had seen him play alongside talents like Laudrup, Gascoigne and Gattuso. The 2002-03 vintage included 1997 Champions League winning goalkeeper Stefan Klos, Dutch international full-back Arthur Numan, Argentina legend Claudio Caniggia, 1995 Champions League winner Ronald De Boer and future Arsenal star Mikel Arteta. It says much about the quality of Scotland's top two teams that a squad featuring such players only won the league on goal difference from a Celtic side that reached the UEFA Cup final.

Celtic regained the title the following season. It was a campaign marred by injuries for Moore, yet, from a personal point of view, it also delivered a significant achievement. After the departure of Barry Ferguson to Blackburn Rovers, manager Alex McLeish named Craig Moore as the club captain.

Moore's injuries kept him out of several fixtures in 2003–04, and the season was a disappointment. Rangers finished 17 points adrift of Celtic in the league and failed to reach even the final of either domestic cup.

Moore's time as club captain was to prove short-lived. The club took a dim view of his decision to play for Australia at the 2004 Olympics when the Games returned to Athens for the first time since 1896. McLeish stripped Moore of the captaincy and put him on the transfer list.

As reported in *The Guardian* on July 9th, 2004, McLeish said, "Each of us has his own objectives, and I have decided to appoint a new captain. I will announce a successor soon. Both Craig and I have agreed the interests of Rangers are the priority, and therefore he will relinquish the captaincy. The club will now make Craig available for transfer at a correct fee."

Only a couple of months beforehand, McLeish had clashed with Moore over the defender questioning the club's ambition ahead of the 2004–05 season.

"It doesn't help for the team captain to come out with this stuff when he is recovering from an operation," McLeish told the *Daily Express* at the time. "I would rather he focused his energy on returning 100% fit and ready to play at a very high standard for us."

Moore's strained relationship with the Rangers boss was the beginning of the end, though McLeish did have to bring the Aussie back into the fold. Ahead of a vital Champions League qualifier at home to CSKA Moscow, he told the press, "I don't want to get involved in the Craig Moore issue and I'm keeping my cards close to my chest. But I think whoever takes the field for Rangers should get 100 per cent backing from the crowd because it is a night when we will need them more than ever."

Rangers were attempting to overcome a 2–1 first-leg deficit, but the Ibrox men could only manage a 1–1 draw in Moore's return to the side.

Although McLeish had suggested Moore was back in contention due to injuries to other players, he continued to select him for several more weeks in a side that was struggling for form. However, the home match against Inverness Caledonian Thistle on September 19th 2004 would prove to be Moore's somewhat anticlimactic Rangers swan song.

With Sean Connery watching from the Ibrox stands, Moore did make a decisive contribution, flicking on a corner to allow Dado Pršo to head in the only goal of what the BBC described as "a nervous 90 minutes for under-pressure Ibrox manager Alex McLeish and his side".

Without Moore, the Gers form would pick up and they eventually regained the league title the following May. By that time, Moore had left Rangers to be reunited with Dick Advocaat at Borussia Monchengladbach in January 2005.

It was a somewhat sad ending to an impressive career at Rangers. The first Aussie to win a Scottish title had played in many memorable Champions League fixtures alongside some world-class talents. With 12 honours to his credit, he would remain the most decorated Aussie player in Scotland for a decade and a half before Tom Rogic edged past him.

Moore was just 29 when he left Rangers for the last time. While the move to Monchengladbach didn't work out, he did end up back in the English Premier League, at Newcastle United, again, following in the footsteps of Dave Mitchell. But injuries prevented Moore from making an impact on Tyneside and he returned to Australia with Brisbane Roar in 2007.

Perhaps his most significant late-career contributions came for the national side as he helped Australia to the last 16 of the World Cup in 2006. There was even a rare goal; his penalty in the group stage match against Croatia would prove important in a 2–2 draw. That result was enough to take them to the knockout rounds. There was even a return to the World Cup finals four years later, when Moore was 34 and helped the Aussies come agonisingly close to a place in the last 16 again.

Today, Moore holds a special place in the hearts of Australian fans and many others on the other side of the planet. Despite the souring of relationships towards the end of the player's tenure at Ibrox, time has allowed fans to appreciate his contribution to the club.

There was even talk of a return as director of football back in 2017. At the time, Moore was director of football at Brisbane Roar, and he was quoted in the *Herald* responding to the rumours of his potential return to Ibrox: "It is obviously extremely flattering to be linked with a club of the size and standing in the game as Rangers."

Ultimately, the rumours would not lead anywhere, but it was an indication that any bad feeling that had lingered over Moore's untidy Ibrox exit had been largely forgiven and forgotten.

At the time of writing, Moore has returned to live in Scotland, where he works as a football agent. The place where he made his name and his home as a teenager is home again.

CHAPTER 4
"You're Staying With Us Now"

"Just before the season started, Dick Advocaat called me into his office and said that the club had to let go of a number of players because the squad was too big and he said that I was free to leave," Tony Vidmar recalled. "He explained that with Arthur Numan coming in and Stale Stensaas still there, they had to let one left-back go. He also said that I had been great in pre-season and he couldn't fault me for anything."

Vidmar's adventure in Scotland had barely got going when it seemed it was about to come to an abrupt end. In his first year at Rangers, the Glasgow giants, with Craig Moore on board, had failed in their bid to achieve 10 titles in a row, which would have broken the tie with Celtic's record of nine. But this blow was compounded by the departures of many of the players who had formed the backbone of the Gers side that had dominated Scottish football for a decade.

Not only had manager Walter Smith decided to move on, but veterans Ally McCoist, Andy Goram, Stuart McCall, Ian Durrant, Richard Gough and Alan McLaren had all either retired or left the club on free transfers. While these players may have been well past their prime, they were not the only departures in a big turnover that summer. Some of the club's finest talent also left Glasgow —Brian Laudrup joined Chelsea, Swedish defender Joachim Bjorklund headed for Valencia and a certain young Italian midfielder called Rino Gattuso returned to his homeland in a transfer to Salernitana. And then Moore was to leave soon after.

While it certainly spelled the end of a very successful era, it wouldn't be long before Ibrox again became home to some world-class talent. But it seemed that Vidmar wasn't part of new boss Advocaat's plans.

"I respected his decision, so for the next two weeks, I was looking for a club," said Vidmar. "It was early to mid-August, but nothing was happening and then Arthur Numan got injured. I got a call asking me to return to first-team training—I'd been training with the second team at that point. I ended up playing that weekend.

"So I went from not being involved to being thrown in at the deep end, and probably played one of my best games. I kept training and on the Monday or Tuesday after the match, I went to Advocaat's office. I reminded him that he had told me I was free to leave. I asked him to put it in writing, just to make it official to facilitate my next move.

"But he said, 'you're staying with us now'. I wasn't complaining about it but it's funny how quickly things can turn around in football. You go from being surplus to requirements to doing something well and they can't let you go. I played about 40 games that season."

The injury to Numan was one of those footballing moments that changed the course of someone else's career and life. It also meant that another Socceroo could make his own memorable contribution to Scottish football.

Vidmar had already made his way to Europe before heading to Glasgow, and he was at a later stage in his career when he arrived in Scotland, compared to most of the Aussies who came before and after him. There had been a short loan spell in Belgium, in 1993, with Germinal Beerschot (Germinal Ekeren at the time), but Vidmar returned to Adelaide City for a further two seasons before heading back to northern Europe.

This time, he was off to the Netherlands, where he became a first-team regular at Eredivisie side NAC Breda. This was where he caught the eye of Rangers when his contract was running out.

"It was early in January, and we were all on our mid-season winter break," Vidmar recalled. "My agent was Tom Van Dalen at that time, and we had an offer to stay on at NAC Breda, but there wasn't really too much of a discussion going on. At that point, the Bosman ruling [which banned restrictions on foreign EU players within national leagues and allowed players in the EU to move to another club at the end of a contract] had taken effect and I was coming to the end of my contract.

"We had the option of not signing on at the club and then being a free agent. I reckon it was the first game after the winter break, maybe late January, my agent had been in touch with some clubs, and a few were interested, including

Borussia Monchengladbach and Glasgow Rangers.

"Tom asked me if I wanted him to let me know if clubs were coming to watch me. And I told him I would like to know who was coming. He said that Monchengladbach were interested but that Rangers wanted to come and see me that weekend.

"I think that first game back was against Sparta Rotterdam, away, which was normally a tough game. It was also the first game back after a break. I think Walter Smith came to that one and I played well in defence that day and tried to keep everything as simple as possible. That Sunday night, my agent called to confirm that Rangers were interested and wanted me to fly to Glasgow on Tuesday to discuss signing a contract. I didn't know how that was going to work, as we had a double training session on Tuesdays. The plan was to fly in on Tuesday afternoon and have the discussions on Wednesday, which was a day off for me.

"I spoke to the manager at NAC to see if I could take the afternoon training session off and I was honest with him. I said that I was looking to sign a contract with another club. He wasn't going to continue the following season either, and he just said that he understood my situation and that he didn't want to stop me from going there.

"So I flew into Glasgow on Tuesday evening, and on that Wednesday, we had the contract discussions, which went pretty quickly. I didn't have to think about it for too long. I had a positive meeting in the morning with Walter, and that Wednesday afternoon, I had agreed to a deal to sign for Rangers."

Nowadays, it would be debatable whether moving from the Dutch top tier to Scotland's Premier League was a step up in quality, but moving from midtable NAC Breda to a club that was a regular fixture in the UEFA Champions League certainly represented a significant jump in the size of the club Vidmar was joining.

Well aware that he was signing for a giant of the European game, he had no hesitation in making the move across the North Sea. He was also under no illusions about the scale of the challenge ahead.

"Walking into a stadium like Ibrox and knowing the club's history was quite intimidating," said Vidmar. "Scottish football was in good health at the time. There were a lot of good players and Rangers were looking to add more new players to the squad for the following season. Because Rangers had a number of injuries when I was negotiating a deal with them, they were interested in bringing me to the club straight away. But I don't think they could come to an agreement with NAC Breda.

"I knew Craig Moore because we were in the national team. He was very helpful at the beginning. He was a young kid trying to make his mark, and I leaned on him a little for some support. I knew it was going to be difficult and had to prepare for it."

While Vidmar had established himself as a regular starter in the Netherlands, he had a battle on his hands to win a place in the Rangers starting XI. The club was enjoying an unprecedented period of domestic success, and it took time and a near exit before Vidmar became a valued member of the team.

"I had to wait for my chance, and I had to take my chance when it came," he said. "That's the way it works at a club of that size. I learned a lot in that first year. When an opportunity presents itself, you've got to take it. Every day at training, you've got to be at your best.

"In my first season, a number of players were ahead of me. They also signed Ståle Stensaas from Rosenborg, so I was in direct competition with him for the left-back position. He was picked ahead of me, which was fine. When there were injuries or another player's form dipped, then I had to be ready to take my opportunity.

"I played a few games but not as many as I was hoping to get in that first season. But I had come into the club and signed a four-year contract and I knew that first 12 months was going to be about getting used to the style of football and Glasgow as a city as well."

But, unlike for most of the previous decade, not everything was going smoothly on the pitch for Rangers, and Celtic were pushing them all the way in the league. The announcement that Walter Smith was to leave came in October 1997, with the bulk of the campaign still to come. Vidmar suggested that the news made players nervous about what a new era would mean for them.

"It was weird because Walter had announced less than halfway through the season that he wasn't going to carry on," said Vidmar. "When Dick Advocaat was confirmed as the new manager shortly afterwards, a lot of players became uncertain about their futures under the new boss. And that uncertainty probably affected how we played.

"As the season came to an end, they started to announce the names of players who were coming in. The squad became big, and you didn't really know where you stood. It was more waiting and seeing how things were in pre-season.

"The quality of players that he brought in, and the ones that he kept, meant the training sessions were so good. There were lots of international players in the prime years of their careers. This allows you to get to know yourself better and to be able to improve your game. You could sense that something special was going to happen that season.

"In the first 12 months I was there, we had Brian Laudrup and Paul Gascoigne. Unfortunately, Gazza had a number of injury problems that season, so we never really saw the best of him, but what we did see was fantastic. We also had Jorg Albertz, and then the following season, we brought in Arthur Numan, Giovanni Van Bronckhorst, Rod Wallace, Gabriel Amato … the list goes on. There were some unbelievable players."

After just about surviving the cull of players who were no longer required by the new manager, Vidmar remembered just how strong the mentality of the team became: "That season, we just developed a sense of belief that meant every time we set foot on the pitch, we knew we were going to win the game. It wasn't arrogance, just confidence and belief in how we played. There was great quality in the squad, and very good understanding between the players."

Vidmar's reprieve had come as a result of the injury to Numan—a player who had just been part of the Netherlands squad that reached the semi-final of the 1998 World Cup. Numan had been first choice, though missed that semi-final through suspension. Having a player of that calibre come to Rangers suggested that Vidmar's second season might be just as challenging as the first, in terms of making himself an indispensable member of the starting XI.

Vidmar did not see things that way. "I am never discouraged. I just think 'alright, it's a challenge'. I like it. You're training with fantastic players and you've got to rise to that. I felt that my game that season was pretty good. It was either sink or swim. My attitude was that I didn't care who they threw at me. In training, I was up against Andrei Kanchelskis every day, and I loved it because I knew he was always going to be at his best.

"With Numan there, and Van Bronckhorst, who sometimes played at left-back, it never fazed me. And at one point, Advocaat put me in the right-back position. Numan was back, and the boss thought I had performed well, so he kept me in the starting XI. Later on, I sometimes played as a centre-back because he knew what he was going to get from me, and that was encouraging."

Having firmly established himself as an important player for Advocaat, Vidmar would soon have the opportunity to win some trophies as well.

With four matches of the season still to go, Rangers had the opportunity to clinch the league title with a victory at Celtic Park. Defeat, on the other hand, would give their rivals some hope and perhaps make the Gers nervous. For Vidmar, there was only going to be one outcome, inspired by two of Lachlan Armstrong's former teammates at Dundee. Even so, there was more drama than Vidmar imagined there might be.

"You go to play your crosstown rivals in their backyard with the opportunity to become the champions there," he recalled. "For us, it was never in doubt. We knew that throughout the season, we had played some great football. We had players who knew how to manage the game and stay calm in key moments. And they weren't. They lost the plot and the occasion got to them.

"The game was chaotic, the referee Hugh Dallas was hit by a coin, there were a few red cards. For us, it was meant to be. Neil McCann had the time of his life, and Billy Dodds was fantastic. The first goal was from a penalty given for a foul against me. We just needed that first goal and from then, we knew we would see it out."

A 3-0 win for Rangers earned Vidmar his first winner's medal at the club, and there would soon be another one. The Aussie played the whole of the Scottish Cup final when the Gers again beat Celtic—this time 1-0 in more sedate circumstances.

Vidmar became used to being a part of one of world football's most intense rivalries—and relished it. Despite the animosity it sometimes generates, he recognises the positive sides.

"You can't explain it. It's something special. You're not prepared for it. You're only prepared once you've been involved in it. You'd love to have games like that every week, but they take their toll on you because they are so demanding, physically and mentally. In the week leading into it, the city is abuzz. There were some great games.

"I had a friend over from Australia for one of the Old Firm games, and he had experienced the derby in Milan. After the game, he said the Milan derby didn't compare, and that this was so much better. At that time, Italian football was the best in the world, so for him to say that was so much better than the Milan derby says something about the rivalry."

After a very successful domestic campaign in 1998-99, Vidmar would soon enjoy the moment for which he is best remembered by Rangers fans.

Having finished second in the Scottish Premier League in 1998, Rangers had been in the unusual position of sitting out the Champions League the following season. However, a victory over Bayer Leverkusen in the UEFA Cup was an indication of the Ibrox side's potential in Europe, even though they bowed out in the last 16 against eventual champions Parma.

The Italians would soon be reunited with the Scots in a playoff for the 1999-2000 Champions League group stages. While Rangers had a strong squad, Parma were the clear favourites, given their pedigree and the quality they possessed. But Fabio Cannavaro's first-half red card in the first leg opened the door for Rangers. Vidmar opened the scoring as the underdog hosts won 2-0. A determined rearguard action in Italy meant Parma could only win the second leg 1-0, with the Scottish side prevailing over two matches. Vidmar's goal remains iconic.

"Every anniversary, I get messages from supporters about that goal," said Vidmar. "It was early in the season, and Parma's season hadn't started yet. So, at home, we felt we had a bit of an advantage. But they had some great players—Gianluigi Buffon in goal, Lilian Thuram, Diego Fuser, Fabio Cannavaro.

"The atmosphere of the Old Firm games is amazing, and then for the Champions League nights, it's on another level. There is a different feeling outside the stadium and out on the pitch. You had to rise to that kind of occasion.

"All I can remember is that the ball came out to me on the left. I cut inside and had a natural instinct just to hit the ball hard. It took a deflection to take it over Buffon and what a moment it was. I didn't score too many goals—I think that was my first for the club. To score it in a Champions League game against Parma is something that I'm never going to forget. It's nice to be a part of history that the Rangers supporters still remember.

"It was something special to beat them 2-0 because they were such a good team. They were ready for the second leg, so for us to only lose 1-0 was a great result. And I hit the crossbar in that one, so it could have been two in two games."

Buoyed by that result, Rangers looked like they had a strong enough squad to make an impact in that season's tournament. However, the draw was not kind—they ended up in the same group as an emerging Valencia side, European powerhouse Bayern Munich and Dutch giant PSV Eindhoven.

Rangers managed to take a respectable seven points from their six matches, but it was only enough for third place behind Valencia and Bayern.

"We definitely felt that we could have got out of the group," said Vidmar. "It was a fantastic Valencia team that we played against. It was always going to be challenging but I think that we did enough to get out of the group—we just didn't capitalise on some opportunities."

Rangers domestic dominance continued in the 1999–2000 season. They finished 21 points clear of second-placed Celtic in the Premier League and sealed a double with a 4–0 drubbing of Aberdeen in the Scottish Cup final. For Vidmar, there was the bonus of another important goal: His thumping strike—Rangers' second—all but ended the Dons' resistance in the cup final.

Despite all that, Rangers' dominance was coming to an end. After seeing their rivals lift 11 titles in 12 years, Celtic brought in a manager with the credentials to shift the balance of power back to the east end of Glasgow. Martin O'Neill joined the Bhoys after a successful spell at Leicester City, and Vidmar knew that Rangers had a rival of substance once again.

"You knew from what he had achieved beforehand that he would definitely have Celtic well organised and make them difficult to beat. The rivalry definitely went to another level, and that's what you want—you had two good sides going toe-to-toe for the championship."

It was from the many tough fixtures between Rangers and Celtic that Vidmar found one of his biggest challenges—going up against Henrik Larsson, a Swede considered by many to be the finest foreign player to grace the Scottish game. Just as the striker had found Craig Moore very difficult to play against, Vidmar thought Larsson gave him some of his most demanding days at the office.

"I had my hardest moments in the games that I played as a centre-back, so Henrik Larsson was one of my toughest opponents," said Vidmar. "He was always in and around where I was. He was difficult because he was a clever player. One minute, you knew where he was but the next minute, he had disappeared and was in another area of the pitch. In and around the box, he had an unbelievable jump to score goals with his head.

"I think on one or two occasions, I also played against Mark Viduka, and it's always special when you play against your fellow countrymen."

National-team commitments are commonplace today but international fixtures were one of the biggest challenges of coming from the other side of the world in Vidmar's day. In 2001, Dick Advocaat was not particularly happy about disruption to his club plans.

"Most of the Australia games were in the FIFA windows," Vidmar recalled. "From 1997 to 1999, we weren't away too much. I reckon in 2000, the games came at the end of the season, so there was no impact.

"In April 2001, we had qualifiers in Australia and it was coming towards the end of the Scottish season. I don't know why we had to go because it was outside the FIFA window, and Advocaat wasn't happy because we still had four to five games of the season left. He was looking at the fixtures and seeing Fiji, American Samoa... He was thinking 'what are these games?' We explained that they were World Cup qualifiers and we had to go.

"We played the games in Coffs Harbour on the east coast, which is well away from Sydney. I think we were away for two-and-half weeks. But the boss wasn't happy about it. I think that was the only time it happened.

"After those games, I asked when he wanted me back for pre-season, and he told me he wanted me back right at the start, and I wasn't getting a holiday."

While Vidmar can reflect on a stint in Scotland that saw him play alongside and against some world-class talents, almost a quarter of a century later, the landscape has changed dramatically.

"Back then, there were some good young players coming through at Celtic and Rangers and other clubs," he said. "There was a good mix of local players and foreign players. But things have changed a lot and the quality isn't there anymore.

"The competition definitely deserves to have really good foreign players because that raises standards. You can see how Barry Ferguson developed at Rangers as an example. He was training with all these great players and that's how he got better. Training with top players is key to development.

"Back then, there was talk about Rangers and Celtic joining the English Premier League, but I don't think that discussion is relevant anymore because of where the two teams are at in terms of quality."

While Vidmar could count Rino Gattuso, a future World Cup winner, among his Rangers colleagues, one French player who had just won the World Cup turned out to be the most notable disappointment.

"Stephane Guivarc'h was a World Cup winner and had come to us from Newcastle United. He found it difficult. I'm not sure if he struggled because of the lifestyle or the football but a player of his quality didn't set the world on fire and he didn't last too long—I think it was only about six months in the end. But that happens. It just didn't work out for him.

"But there weren't too many failures. In that first season at Rangers, Jonas Thern came from Roma. I thought he was a quality player. When I joined, Gattuso was already there, and starting to develop into a top player. Within a few seasons, he was the focal point of the team at AC Milan. We had so many good players. In goals, we even had two top keepers in Stefan Klos and Antti Niemi."

In 2002, at the age of 32, it was time for Vidmar to move away from Ibrox. At that point, Rangers may have seen Celtic win two titles in a row, but the Aussie bowed out with a couple of winners medals. Vidmar was on from the start as the Gers defeated Ayr United 4-0 in the Scottish League Cup final. However, he stayed on the bench as he watched them beat their biggest rivals 3-2 in that year's Scottish Cup final.

"I had a fantastic time at every club I went to," he said. "But at Rangers, I spent five unbelievable years and it was by far the best experience I had as a player. When you walk through the main doors at Ibrox, it just sends shivers through you. I went there not knowing too much about Scottish football, so learning about the history was another part of the enjoyment.

"I learned a lot about the size of Rangers the first season I was there. We had an internal training match one or two weeks before the start of the season at Ibrox. It was sold out. How do you explain that to people? It's insane."

In his five-year spell at Rangers, the team went from having a Scottish core, topped up by some foreign talent, to becoming a mix of many nations. Not only did it change the way the team operated on the park, it also had an impact on the social side of things.

"I think towards the end of my time there, the mixture of foreign players changed the way we socialised," said Vidmar. "We often had nights out and we'd bump into the Celtic players and people would find that strange. As time went on, it became the norm.

"It had a lot to do with there being a lot of foreign players who had something in common despite playing for rival clubs."

As well as being a professional football player, Vidmar had something else in common with a player who arrived in Glasgow in 1999, though his fellow Australian was joining the club on the other side of the city.

"When Mark Viduka joined Celtic, I sent him a message because I wanted to catch up with him, to help him settle in and see if there was anything he needed as I had been in Glasgow for a year and a half. So me and my wife went out for dinner with Mark and his wife.

"The next day in training, two of the Scottish boys asked what I had done the previous night. I told them I had been out for dinner. They asked who I went out with and I said Mark Viduka. They said, 'Don't you ever do that again'.

"I could understand where they were coming from but I didn't see it that way. He was a fellow countryman and he was a mate. In my second year at Rangers, there must have been about 12 to 15 foreign players, and we went out together. It was normal to meet the Celtic players. None of the players saw it as an issue. Giovanni Van Bronckhorst and Henrik Larsson were best of mates, and they hung out together a lot."

The Glasgow rivalry has left a lasting impression on Vidmar, as has the Scottish game in general. Thanks to that goal against Parma, Vidmar has left a lasting impression on the Scottish game. Considering that Dick Advocaat was happy to let him leave in the summer of 1998, that's quite an achievement.

CHAPTER 5
The One-Season Wonder

"Mark Viduka was one of Australia's finest soccer players ... In Viduka's one and a half seasons with Celtic, he made 37 appearances and scored 30 goals in the Scottish Premier League. In his full season at Celtic, ... Viduka took out the golden boot with 27 goals and was named the Professional Footballers' Association Scotland's Players' Player of the Year, making him the first player from outside of Europe to win the award."

Sport Australia's Hall of Fame entry for Mark Viduka certainly highlights the impact the striker made in his short spell in Scotland, but opinion on his time at Celtic is forever tainted by an incident that took place on February 8th, 2000. Celtic Park was the scene of Inverness Caledonian Thistle's legendary 3-1 victory in the Third Round of the Scottish Cup.

It wasn't a case of a big club being complacent because their priorities lay elsewhere. This was a Celtic side that had just suffered a humiliating home loss, surrendering a 2-0 lead to slip to a 3-2 defeat to Hearts. That result effectively ended their hopes of winning the league title, so the Scottish Cup had to take priority for manager John Barnes.

Just three days later, Inverness would inflict further pain on the Bhoys and put Barnes out of a job. In the weeks and months that followed that humiliating result, it became apparent that a half-time incident in the Celtic Park dressing room had seen Viduka decide he'd had enough.

With Celtic 2-1 down at the halfway stage, Ian Wright had to make an appearance as a substitute. But the Arsenal legend was not brought on for tactical reasons or to replace an injured player. What had taken place was much more unusual.

Ian Wright told Ball Street, "Mark Viduka refused to play in the second half. It's a nightmare that one, and it's one that I always feel really uncomfortable with. I remember at the time everyone was getting a lot of stick. He came in at half-time, took his boots off and said, 'fuck this'.

"We couldn't believe it. It was the first time I had ever seen it. I thought it was a disgrace. I remember leaving the ground that night and we had to have a police escort because Celtic fans obviously went crazy. When Mark Viduka went out, they actually cheered him."

What Wright failed to realise is that the fans had no idea what had happened in the dressing room. The Celtic supporters had assumed that the striker had been replaced due to an injury. The truth leaked out in dribs and drabs over time, but that night, the fans were angry with the team, but oblivious to Viduka's remarkable tantrum.

It took 20 years for Viduka to break his silence on the incident, and in an interview with The World Game in 2020, he recalled Celtic's assistant coach Eric Black having a go at him at the break, with Celtic losing to a team from the lower tier: "So what happened was I walked in at half time and the assistant coach sort of questioned me.

"He basically said 'what's up big fella, do you not fancy it today?' And something in my head just clicked because that's the type of guy I am, and I just lost it. I said to him 'If I'm not good enough to play, then put someone else on'."

Celtic midfielder Paul Lambert was in the stadium that night, but he was having a cup of tea with Henrik Larsson when Viduka was throwing in the towel.

Lambert said, "Me and Henrik were injured that night and we were sitting together in the stand. Inverness scored first, we equalised, and then they got a second to lead at half-time.

"During the break, me and Henrik went down to have a cup of tea in the laundry room. Some of the players used to hang about there and have a chat with wee Angie, the woman who worked there.

"We heard shouting and arguing coming from the dressing room. We didn't go in as we weren't playing, but we just thought that was normal when the team wasn't playing well.

"When we sat down for the second half, we noticed that big Mark wasn't there, and Ian Wright had replaced him. We thought Mark must have been injured as he was our main goalscorer. We thought nothing of it at the time, but after the game we realised that he had said he wasn't going to play.

"I was never privy to exactly what happened. You hear different versions. Maybe Mark thought he was being unfairly criticised, but that was him. He had a temperamental side. I'm sure he had his reasons for doing it. But from then on, it didn't seem to bother him. The incident didn't weigh on him. Other players might have crumbled in front of the Celtic fans as they tried to come back from that, but he just got on with it.

"He had scored against Rangers a few weeks earlier, so that would have given him some credit with the Celtic fans. Looking back, was he right to do what he did? No, he wasn't."

It would certainly be unfair to suggest that this one incident defined his time at Celtic Park, and Lambert has fond memories of Viduka the player and Viduka the man.

The striker first came on the radar of Celtic's players and fans when he played a starring role for Croatia Zagreb in a playoff for entry to the group stage of the 1998-99 UEFA Champions League. The Zagreb side had plenty of gifted players, and Viduka made a lasting impression.

Lambert said, "We played them at Celtic Park in the first leg and beat them 1-0, but it was one of those games when we rode our luck somewhat. They had Robert Prosinecki, who was a top player, as well as Dario Simic, Silvio Maric and several other players who had been in the Croatia squad that came third at that year's World Cup in France. I think a lot of them ended up moving to some of Europe's top sides after we played them.

"They were a really good side, and we had a really hard time in the return leg, which they won 3-0. Viduka and Maric were up front for them and gave our centre-backs a tough time.

"When he signed, all the lads remembered him from his performance that night so we were quite excited as we knew that we were getting a really talented striker.

"I knew Australia was emerging as a football nation, and several players were coming through and playing in Europe. I think there were a few in Germany and England. But Viduka's journey was different as he'd gone to Croatia, and I'm sure that was a tough league to play in."

If there was drama on that night against Inverness, there would be drama before Viduka could even make his Celtic debut. Sport Australia's Hall of Fame entry states, "Viduka's move to Celtic was delayed when he walked out just four days after signing due to stress. He refreshed himself back on home soil before continuing his career at Celtic."

It was one of those transfer sagas that dragged on and had Celtic fans questioning their new signing's commitment to the cause. It didn't help, therefore, that the Inverness episode came less than a year on from that delay.

In a 2020 interview with ESPN, Viduka admitted, "I was burned out. Burned out mentally. I just needed a break, and getting back to see my family and friends is what I needed. Thank God I did. They (Celtic) were understanding but urged me back. I have a lot to thank them for."

Football fans are very forgiving when a player delivers on the pitch, and it didn't take long for Viduka to show his quality when he finally got his Celtic career up and running. In the quarter-final of the 1999 Scottish Cup, he scored a memorable first goal for the club in the unglamorous surroundings of Greenock Morton's Cappielow Park stadium.

With his back to goal just inside the penalty area, he bamboozled a defender with a Cruyff turn, and nonchalantly fired a shot into the top corner with the outside of his right foot. It was the type of goal that highlighted his mercurial talent, and he would go on to score countless more spectacular strikes throughout his career.

It certainly gave fans reassurance that this was a player who had been worth the wait. He scored a second goal that evening, and he would become a prolific goal scorer for the next 12 months.

The qualities seen in that first goal were similar to the qualities highlighted by Lambert when he remembered Viduka's main strengths: "Big Mark was brilliant with his back to goal and, overall, he was just an unbelievable talent. He was brilliant with both feet and could turn defenders or hold the ball up. When he put his mind to it, he was unplayable.

"For me as a midfielder, he was brilliant to play with as the ball would just stick to him. You knew that defenders couldn't move him because he was that big, and used his arms and his backside really well.

"You knew if you wanted to play a one-two with Viduka, the ball was coming back to you. His touch never let him down. He was really good at the Cruyff turn as well.

"He wasn't the type of player to run in the channels and press hard, but if you aimed the right ball at him, he could hold onto it and bring other players into the game. I can't remember seeing him getting pushed off the ball. And his finishing was top drawer.

"He could score goals out of nothing. I remember him doing the Cruyff turn to make space for one of his goals, and he was good at all types of finishes."

Following that double at Morton, Viduka struck four times in four league matches. He also netted in the Scottish Cup semi-final win over Dundee United. Title hopes had pretty much been extinguished before Viduka's arrival, so the cup was their last chance of a trophy that season. Unfortunately, along with several teammates, he missed the final due to injury as the Bhoys lost 1-0 to Rangers.

By then, fans and teammates had seen what the Aussie was capable of. He was one of those players whose skill set did not quite fit his physique. He was 6ft 2in tall and had an extremely powerful build. He looked more like the kind of striker whose main strengths would be to win the physical battle with defenders and find a range of finishes—a striker in the mould of Alan Shearer. Instead, he had the physique of Shearer combined with the light touch of Dennis Bergkamp. His touch could be exquisite, and his skills were more like those of a playmaker than a target man.

With the benefit of a full preseason with the squad, fans could look forward to the 1999-2000 season with optimism. Viduka and Larsson looked set to form a formidable front pairing.

It was all looking so good—until fate intervened.

Now under the management of John Barnes, Celtic kicked off the season with a 5-0 victory at Aberdeen, Viduka and Larsson netting two apiece. They had scored 10 goals between them in the first seven league matches, before they faced Aberdeen again.

At Celtic Park, the strikers each scored a hat-trick in a 7-0 trouncing of the hapless Dons. Celtic had taken 21 out of the first 24 points of the season and were well on course to mount a stronger title challenge.

But then came the match in Lyon, where the wheels came off.

It was the first leg of a second-round UEFA Cup clash. Larsson suffered a horrendous leg break, which pretty much ended his season as early as October 21st. He may have been just one player, but his importance to the team could be measured in how quickly things fell apart after his injury.

Celtic actually won their next league game to stay within a point of Rangers at the top, but then lost three of the following five. This meant the December clash at home to Rangers felt like a must-win. A fine Viduka strike opened the scoring, but the Gers soon equalised, and the match finished 1-1.

Six weeks later, the defeat to Hearts and then there was the ignominy against Inverness...

Viduka scored four times in the three games that followed that debacle, but the goals would dry up towards the end of the campaign. The striker did lift a trophy when Celtic defeated Aberdeen 2–0 in the League Cup final, but it felt slightly hollow given the traumas of the league challenge and the Inverness calamity.

The season ended with rumours swirling around about Viduka's future, and he was soon on his way to Leeds United despite new boss Martin O'Neill's attempts to persuade him to stay. Lambert saw this as a missed opportunity to become a Celtic great: "If he had stayed at Celtic for longer and kept performing at the level he was capable of, he would have been Henrik's strike partner and that would have been some partnership.

"Mark could have gone down in history as one of Celtic's greatest strikers. Because he wasn't at the club for very long, the fans might not have the clearest memory of him, but he left a big impression on all of the players he played with at the club.

"He was a brilliant guy. He was funny. He never caused any problems with any players in the dressing room. He wasn't moody. He's the type of guy who, if I met him today, I'm sure we would sit down and have a laugh like we'd known each other for years."

A niggling thought remains with Lambert, as it does with many who followed Viduka's career. Just how good could he have been?

"I can't help thinking that he should have done better in his career than he actually did," said Lambert. "I know he played in the English Premier League for Leeds United, Middlesbrough and Newcastle United, but I thought he could have achieved more with the talent he had.

"His career was on an upward trajectory at Leeds, and I think the move to Middlesbrough maybe wasn't the best one for him. I can see similarities with Dimitar Berbatov in terms of his skill levels."

Lambert knows a thing or two about top strikers, having played alongside Larsson, Chris Sutton and John Hartson at Celtic, as well as Karl-Heinz Riedle and Stephane Chapuisat at Borussia Dortmund.

"He's up there," said Lambert of Viduka. "Absolutely no question about it. Like those guys, when he went through on goal, one-to-one with the goalkeeper, you were very confident he would find the finish. You can't say that about too many strikers.

"He was really laid back and maybe that just kept him from pushing on.

When I heard that he was now running a coffee shop, that didn't surprise me at all. It seemed to fit his personality."

Golden Boot, Player of the Year, a player whose talents left a big impression on those he played with and against. But Viduka's Celtic legacy is a complicated one because of its brevity and that night he refused to play back in February 2000.

Of all the Socceroos who have played in Scotland, he was almost certainly the most talented. He just didn't stick around long enough to give himself a shot at being the most successful.

CHAPTER 6

The Agent

In 1984, Dave McPherson had a bruising introduction to football in Australia. At the age of 20, he was part of the Rangers squad that travelled Down Under as part of a world tour.

McPherson said, "We played against the Australian A team and B team. There must have been about nine matches in all. There were some quite physical encounters, and Rangers picked up a number of injuries. These kinds of trips wouldn't happen anymore …"

It wasn't actually McPherson's first match against an Aussie side. The previous year, he had come up against Australia while playing for Scotland in the FIFA World Youth Championship in Mexico. His future friend Fabio Incantalupo was on target in a 2–1 victory for the Young Socceroos that day. A decade and a half would pass before McPherson started to build the connections that would see him make a major impact on the careers of some promising young Australian talents.

He recalls playing with Dave Mitchell at Ibrox in the early part of his career, and it was an early indication of the characteristics that he would come to recognise in the majority of players from the country.

"Dave was quite physical, strong and athletic," said McPherson. "I wouldn't have said he was the most skilful of players, but he would admit that himself. Like all Australians in sport, he always gave it 100 percent."

While Mitchell's stay at Rangers was relatively brief, McPherson's relationship with him has endured. To this day, they cross paths professionally as both continue working in football in their early 60s.

"We got on well. I actually spoke to him recently," said McPherson. "I was back in Australia when an American University was visiting Sydney and Dave was organising some games for them. We still have links together through the work we do."

While McPherson and Mitchell played together early in their careers, it was only when McPherson was looking for a change of scenery at the end of his time as a player that he really became involved with football in Australia.

The defender had enjoyed a fine career that featured two spells at Rangers and two stints at Hearts. He won three league titles and several domestic cups at the Gers, while also lifting the Scottish Cup with Hearts in 1998.

A year after that triumph, he decided that it was time for something new at the age of 35. A call from a former Rangers teammate meant that something new would be Carlton SC in Australia's National Soccer League. That kick-started a journey that would see McPherson lead many young Aussies in the opposite direction.

Stuart Munro had played alongside McPherson at Rangers in the 1980s, and had become manager at Carlton SC. Munro felt that his old friend had something valuable to offer.

"I was getting to that age at the end of my career when I wanted to try something different, so I was looking at options abroad," said McPherson. "I had a chance to go to Austria, but then Stuart phoned me and told me I should come to Melbourne, which I had been to before, but a long time ago. He said it was a great city, with great weather, and that it was a bit more laidback.

"I just thought I should go for it. The fact that it was English-speaking was another appealing factor. I wasn't averse to learning a new language, but the fact that it was English-speaking would just make it that bit easier rather than moving to Austria."

Australia made a very positive impression on McPherson but off-field issues at the club created unwanted drama.

"I loved it there," he said. "The only problem was the volatility at the clubs as they were all franchise-owned. There was a history of them starting up and then going to the wall, and that's what happened at Carlton. The owners were putting money in but as soon as they stopped investing, things fell apart. That was a disappointing part of it because a lot of work had been done there in terms of building from grassroots up."

Despite the setbacks that were the result of financial mismanagement, McPherson threw himself into the experience at Carlton. It gave him a taste for helping to develop young talent, and raised awareness of a potential market for his future role.

"At the time, I just wanted to go out there and enjoy the experience. I got involved in a lot of coaching with younger players, including Archie Thompson. I went to do a bit of coaching in a lot of primary schools because they were trying to spread the word about soccer being the number one sport in the world. Because I was a marquee player, I was asked to go out to different schools throughout the Melbourne and Victoria area, and it was something I was quite happy to do.

"Through doing that, I learned that there was a lot of interest in the English Premier League, the Scottish league and some of the big European leagues."

While McPherson was getting a taste for coaching, he was also building a network within Australian football. This was not done with any great sense of purpose, it just developed naturally through the work he was doing and the people he was meeting.

When he returned to Scotland to play for Greenock Morton in 2001, he was also handed the role of assistant manager. The following year, he took the opportunity to become player-manager but it was a short-lived appointment.

McPherson soon saw his future elsewhere. He became an agent, almost by accident. He recalled, "I made a lot of good contacts in Australia at the management and coaching level, not just at club level, but also with the international teams and the Institute of Sport. Once I went back to Scotland, a lot of people got in touch to say they were interested in coming over and trying to get an opportunity.

"Australia was producing a lot of good young players, and coaches were telling me that they had some very promising players who wanted to go to the UK. It started off with them asking if I could help out, and I was happy to do it. I just fell into the role. Once I got one player fixed up, the floodgates opened, and everybody seemed to want to come over.

"One thing that made it easier was that a lot of these players had passports for a European country, so there was never really a problem with the visas.

"I dealt with many people in Australia at the time, but the main ones were Stuart Munro and Fabio Incantalupo, who was a coach at Carlton. The interesting thing about Fabio was that I had actually played against him at the 1983 FIFA World Youth Championship in Mexico. So there was a connection going way back."

While there was a lot of interest, finding the players who would reach the highest level of the game would prove very challenging. The players who stood out in their younger days were not always the best equipped for a move to the UK.

"There were a few who came over and did reasonably well, including Scott Tunbridge and Matthew Ryan (not the goalkeeper)," said McPherson. "There were also several players who were really good at the academy level but never really made it to the top level.

"Patrick Kisnorbo was about the first one to come over and do really well. I had played against him when he was at South Melbourne and Ange Postecoglou was the manager there. I knew what he was like as a player, and he was looking for a chance to play in the UK.

"When he first arrived in Scotland, I took him for a training session at a place in Edinburgh called The Meadows. It was a 90-minute session, and I don't think he'll ever forget—a bit of Scottish fitness."

Kisnorbo made his breakthrough at McPherson's former club Hearts and would go on to have successful spells at Leicester City and Leeds United. But there were other players who would make a bigger and more sustained impression in Scotland.

"The main ones who reached a higher level were Scott McDonald, Ryan McGowan, Dylan McGowan and Patrick," said McPherson. "Scott had another manager in 2004 and I was asked to help him get a move, and I managed to get him an opportunity at Motherwell as they were managed by Terry Butcher, who is a good friend of mine. And Scott did really well for him there.

"Stuart Munro had managed Scott at Gippsland Falcons in Melbourne before he joined Carlton. Stuart managed him as a young boy, and he told me that he was one to look out for—he was a goal scorer. He wasn't the biggest, but he was stocky, and Stuart fancied him to do well.

"Things went quiet for a while, but Stuart got in touch again to tell me he was looking for a new opportunity, and that was when I managed to get him [Scott] to Motherwell. I wasn't surprised by the success he went on to have because I always trust Stuart Munro's judgement of a player, especially one he has worked with at a young age. Stuart did say that he could develop into a top player."

McPherson suspects that McDonald needed to find the right manager to get the best out of his undoubted ability and, just as importantly, to manage his challenging personality.

"Scott did have a bit of an attitude about him, which either helped or hindered him," said McPherson. "Some managers liked it but others probably didn't get on with him. I know that Terry found him a handful, but he scored goals. So when you've got a bit of arrogance, it's okay if you can back it up."

McDonald would move on to hit new heights at Celtic, but McPherson was starting to consider getting out of the role of agent.

"I was still involved with Scott when he was at Celtic, and I worked with another agent called Lou Sticca. But this was around the time that I decided I wanted to move away from managing players because there were too many people involved. Earlier in my time as an agent, I had a personal relationship with the players in a one-to-one sense. But it had started growing arms and legs, and everyone wanted a piece of the pie. I didn't like that part of it, which is why I got out when I did."

While McDonald stands out as the pick of the players who McPherson helped earn moves to Scottish clubs, the McGowan brothers have cemented their connection over a long period with multiple clubs.

As of September 2024, Ryan had played for eight Scottish clubs (including three on loan) from his move to Hearts in 2008 to his arrival at Livingston 16 years later. Younger brother Dylan also started his career in Scotland at Hearts. He returned after seven years away when he joined Kilmarnock in 2021, and was playing for Hamilton Academical at the age of 33.

McPherson thought highly of both of them and had firm belief in their ability to be successful overseas.

"I think Dylan was actually the better player," he said. "Ryan had a bit more pace, but they were both very good and really good lads as well. Typical of most Australian players, they were fit and athletic, and you knew they weren't going to let you down.

"I got to know Ryan through a contact at the South Australia Institute of Sport. I knew one of the coaches there and had spoken to him many times. He told me he had a really good young player from Adelaide who was looking to come over to the UK, and I managed to get him a trial at Hearts.

"There was always a chance at Hearts because I had connections there and both Patrick Kisnorbo and Ryan got in and did really well on trial and managed to secure a contract."

For every player who went on to play at the top level in Scotland, there were several that would not have the same impact. It wasn't always clear why, but that has always been the way with younger players.

"There were other players who came through but never really kicked on, and some ended up in Scandinavia or went back to play in Australia," said McPherson. "I thought Scott Tunbridge was a really good player. He had great ability, he was two-footed, he was good in the air, he had a really nice touch, and his movement was good. But he just never kicked on to the next level and ended up going back to Australia.

"There are some players who you just wonder why it doesn't work out because they sometimes have better ability than the ones who reach higher levels. It could just be getting a lucky break at the right time. And, as it's all opinion based, it could be about finding the right manager. Some managers rate you and others don't."

The flood of Australians into Scottish football is logical for McPherson. He sees integration as far more straightforward than it is for some other foreign players.

"I think it's the overall combination of ability, fitness, and attitude. As they're English-speaking, there's never really a problem getting them integrated into the team. They're hard working. They tick a lot of the boxes.

"When one comes over and does well, you're more likely to take a look at some others, and it follows from there. I'm not surprised, and I think there are a lot more players out in Australia who could come over and do well. The main barrier is visas."

While McPherson stopped working as an agent over a decade ago, his role in helping several Aussie players get a foothold at UK clubs hasn't been forgotten.

"I still get requests for help all the time," he said. "I'm actually looking at getting back involved. I was in Melbourne and Sydney this year and they do trials for American universities and every player you meet wants to come over for a trial in the UK. I keep getting asked.

"They sign up with my company to go and study in the USA, but they still want to know if I can help them get a trial. I just need to look into the best way to do that as the players have to fund travel over to the UK, and that's not cheap nowadays."

While McPherson was adept at finding the right clubs for some Aussie players, he doesn't see it being quite as straightforward for any coaches wanting to emulate Ange Postecoglou—a man he has crossed paths with several times.

"Ange was well regarded as a coach," said McPherson. "I remember bumping into him at airports a few times on trips back and forward to Sydney, and he came across really well. He talks about football in a really positive sense. Even in his early days, he had a clear idea of how he wanted to play and how he wanted his teams set up. I could tell that from the time I played against South Melbourne for Carlton. They were a well organised side that looked to score goals.

"But it's such a cut-throat business now that it's all about getting the right job at the right time in management. There are many talented managers and coaches out there—not just in Australia but all over. When I got into management, the first person I spoke to was Walter Smith. The first thing he reminded me of was that the only thing guaranteed in management was the sack.

"You can be a talented manager and have all the best ideas, but if your team doesn't win, your days are numbered. Patrick Kisnorbo went to France [with Troyes], and it didn't work out. You wonder if it was the right choice at the right time. You never know."

Dave McPherson is well known as the skilful defender who enjoyed a trophy-laden career for Rangers and Hearts and as a key man in Scotland sides that played at the World Cup and European Championships. He is less well known as the man who brought Scott McDonald to Scottish football—and his influence on linking Socceroos to Scotland is significant.

CHAPTER 7
The Star Striker

On October 3rd, 2007, Australian striker Scott McDonald is about to play for Celtic against European champions AC Milan in the group stage of the UEFA Champions League in a rain-soaked Glasgow.

"I remember standing in the tunnel and thinking, 'I belong here'. Going up against Nesta, I just thought, 'I'm going to have you early here'. Maybe he didn't know who I was but I wanted him to remember me."

With 89 minutes on the clock, Shunsuke Nakamura receives the ball on the right wing. After a bit of trickery, he feeds the ball into the AC Milan penalty area to Scott Brown. Brown lays the ball off to the edge of the box, where Gary Caldwell is lurking.

Caldwell sidefoots it low towards the corner of the goal. It's not a powerful shot, but Dida has to scramble to his left and manages to keep the ball out. It falls straight into the path of McDonald, and the Australian striker slots the ball into an empty net from six yards out. Celtic have beaten the European champions, and a Socceroo has scored the winning goal.

Alessandro Nesta may have been a two-time Champions League winner and part of the triumphant Italy squad at the 2006 World Cup, but McDonald had no fear of this world-class defender. The Italian star would have cause to remember the Aussie for the last-minute strike that secured the Bhoys an unlikely 2–1 victory. Not only did McDonald net the winner, but he also, as intended, had Nesta 'early'.

"I got booked but it was just to let him know who I was," said McDonald. "I genuinely thought that way. I'm big on mentality and strength of character. It's so huge in influencing what you can achieve, and that was one of those moments. Scoring that goal was a dream come true. There was euphoria. It was just crazy—an amazing moment that people will remember forever and that's quite special for me."

It may have been the biggest moment for McDonald during his time in Scotland, but there were plenty more significant contributions that are remembered to this day for the impact they had. He was certainly a man for the big occasion, but his success did not come easy.

Like many before and after him, McDonald travelled from Australia to England in an attempt to develop his career, but his family had roots in Glasgow—and fate would take him North.

"My mum's side of the family was from Govan, while my dad grew up in the Gorbals and Castlemilk, then moved to East Kilbride before he finally left to emigrate to Australia. They were just happy that I was getting an opportunity to play professional football at a senior level, regardless of the location."

McDonald made a promising start to life in England when he earned a deal with Southampton at just 17. A change of management spelled the end of his time there after just three first-team appearances but there would be an ironic twist in the tale.

The new manager was Gordon Strachan—the man who would go on to have a huge influence on McDonald's career further down the line. After leaving Southampton, the young player endured some difficult moments before he finally reached the destination from which to launch his career.

"It was a tough period before I actually got to Mothwerwell," he said. "I went on trial at numerous places. I was on a month-to-month contract with Wimbledon, so it was a difficult time. I just stuck at it, and Motherwell was pretty much the final opportunity for me.

"If it hadn't worked out at Motherwell, I'd have ended up back in Australia at that point because I had pushed the boundaries quite far, and mentally I was ready to, not give up, but restart everything and have the support of my family. Thankfully, things turned out a little bit differently in the end.

"I had been on trials, and Dave McPherson, who looked after me at the time, advised me to have a trial at Motherwell. I was against it at the time, but then just thought there was nothing to lose. In the end, I agreed to go—and if it didn't work out, I would go home."

Being shown the door at an English Premier League club before enduring a struggle to find another team might have led some players to question if this might not have been the right career for them. McDonald was not one of those players.

"I never lost belief in my ability, I just lost belief in the ability of others to give me a shot," he said. "I was always a cocky little shit, so I was never thinking it was down to me but it was down to others and their opinions.

"Thankfully, Terry Butcher at Motherwell was someone who saw something in me straight away. I think I trained for three days. We played 11 Vs 11 against the first team and I ended up tearing the first team to shreds in that game. The story goes that Stevie Craigan was straight up to the manager at that point and telling him, 'You need to sign him now'.

"I signed about four days later. I was only on about £200 a week, but I didn't care. It was just about playing and becoming part of a first-team squad. And Terry was amazing in terms of giving players belief and giving them the platform to go out and enjoy themselves. He was such a good motivator, and that was exactly what I needed at that point in my career."

Having joined in January 2004, 20-year-old McDonald made a slow start in his first half season, but he really started to make an impact thereafter. He had to wait until the final match of the 2003-04 season to net his first league goal for 'Well after 10 starts and five substitute appearances.

It was a fairly inauspicious beginning. While it did not look like he had hit the ground running if he was going to have a career as a striker, McDonald's goals would directly influence the outcome of the Scottish title within a year. His second-season return was 15 league goals—the sixth highest in the division, which suggested that the slow start was just him settling in.

In a six-game run from late August to early October 2004, McDonald netted seven times as Motherwell took 14 points. It was a season of streaks for the North Lanarkshire club as they took just one point from the next six matches before winning five on the trot and then taking one point from 18 again. McDonald's scoring form was also streaky, but there was a landmark goal on December 27th that year: he scored against Rangers. It was a mere consolation in a 4-1 defeat, but scoring against the Ibrox club would later become a habit.

Motherwell finished the season in indifferent form, even if they stunned Celtic on the final day, putting the name of Scott McDonald firmly in the headlines.

For Celtic supporters of a certain generation, the worst moment of their time following the club came on May 22nd, 2005.

Needing just to beat Motherwell on the final day of the 2004-05 season, Celtic are leading 1-0 with three minutes remaining. Several good chances to seal the game and the title have been squandered, and the visitors to Fir Park are getting the jitters as Richie Foran aims a hopeful shot from long range at the Celtic goal.

Scott McDonald gets in front of Bobo Balde to intercept the weak shot. He controls the ball with his chest and, despite having his back to goal, he swivels and instinctively volleys the ball high into the Celtic net. It is the classic strike out of nothing, and it will have far-reaching consequences.

Two minutes later, with Celtic having committed bodies forward in search of a winner, McDonald strikes again. Not only has the striker denied Celtic the title, he has given it to Rangers.

They are goals that McDonald is still reminded of on a regular basis, and for him, that day was an important stepping stone in his development: "It's a big part of my history and my story. I will always be remembered for that. But if I hadn't scored those goals, I might not have had the platform to go on and play for a club like Celtic.

"I always think that things like that happen for a reason, and that gave me the opportunity to reach a higher level, so I certainly don't have an issue with it."

The 21-year-old striker stayed at Motherwell, but his goal-scoring had caught the eye of other clubs. In the 2005–06 season, he scored a more modest 11 league goals, but it was still a decent total for a team that finished eighth. He also hit the target against Celtic once again—netting once in a chaotic 4-4 draw on Matchday One.

"Motherwell was a fantastic period for me," he recalled. "When I got there, it was a club that was just getting to grips with coming out of administration, trying to build a team again. But we had some really experienced guys, like Scott Leitch, Derek Adams, Gordon Marshall and Phil O'Donnell—players who had had great careers, so it was great to have them to learn from.

"They didn't make it easy for you either, but I came in with a lot of confidence and the team had a decent spell when I was there. We had a couple of top-six finishes, we got to a League Cup final, and I was the club's top scorer on a few occasions. I did really well at the club. I was just enjoying my football at that time. But I did have ambitions, and Motherwell were always a selling club."

Despite scoring almost 30 goals over two seasons for a mid-table side, McDonald would stay at Motherwell for another season as speculation mounted about interest from other clubs, including Celtic and Rangers. Although 'Well endured a dismal start to the 2006–07 campaign, McDonald had netted seven league goals by mid-October as his star continued to rise.

In January 2007, Rangers boss Walter Smith made his move. Despite growing up as a Celtic fan, McDonald was willing to go to Ibrox, even though the Bhoys would have been his first choice. He felt that the wounds his goals had inflicted almost two years earlier would not have healed sufficiently among the Celtic faithful.

"There was a lot of talk, but nothing really happened until Rangers came in the transfer window before Celtic bought me," said McDonald. "That's when things really started to take off. Whether or not there had been conversations before that, I wasn't aware of them. I just played my game and really enjoyed my time there. I've still got really close friends from that Motherwell team. It was a huge part of my growing up, on and off the park. It's a real family club.

"The Rangers move in January 2007 was something I wanted to happen. If you were in my shoes at that point, it just didn't seem likely that Celtic were going to come in for me at any point due to what had happened just 18 months earlier. I never thought that the club would be big enough to look past that no matter who was in charge. But I was wrong, wasn't I?

"But at the time Rangers came in for me, it was a chance to play for a team that would be playing European football and challenging for trophies. It was an opportunity to play at a higher level and get into the national side, so it was a no-brainer in that sense.

"However, the club wouldn't allow the move to go through at that time. I wasn't happy about it but Maurice Malpas, the coach, explained that they had just sold Richie Foran to Southend and losing me would leave them short when relegation was still a threat."

After Motherwell blocked the move to Ibrox, McDonald got his head down and kept up his scoring form, ending the season on 15 league goals again—an even more impressive return considering his team finished in 10th spot. Celtic boss Gordon Strachan had seen enough and, with Rangers hovering again, the Hoops manager and a £700,000 fee took him to Celtic Park.

"In the end, I stuck it out," McDonald recalled. "It didn't affect me, and I continued banging the goals in until the end of the season. But it was odd that I signed for Celtic in March or April. That just doesn't normally happen if you still have 18 months left on your contract. It only happens when players are out of contract and are on a free deal. But Motherwell agreed a fee with Celtic before the end of the season, and I knew I was going, and everyone else at the club knew I was going.

"It was weird but I went out with a carefree attitude, and I was buzzing because I knew I was going to Celtic, but I still wanted to perform for Motherwell."

Despite earning a dream move to the club he had supported as a boy, McDonald felt that many Celtic supporters were reluctant to forgive him for his role in the collapse of the club's title hopes in 2005. Those fears not only highlight the tribal nature of football in Glasgow, but also just how much impact his goals had. One can only imagine what the noise might have been had social media been as prevalent and powerful in 2007 as it is today.

McDonald proved resilient, however. He still had the same self-confidence and determination that had kept him going through some difficult years before Motherwell gave him his first big break.

"A lot of fans didn't want me there," he said. "When I signed, there was plenty of negativity. I went into the cauldron, but I accepted that. I could have gone to Rangers because they kept up their interest in me. I had two offers on the table, and I chose to go to Celtic. I was more than ready to put up with the challenge ahead.

"The fact that some fans didn't welcome me spurred me on. If you're going to doubt me, it's going to inspire me and push me to prove you wrong. I knew from the beginning, I was up against it, so I had to do more than most."

If Scott believed that a section of fans did not want to see him at Celtic Park, he found a key ally in one of the most revered Hoops players of all time. Tommy Burns holds a special place in the hearts of all Celtic fans who watched him during his playing days, and younger fans who have learned of his legendary status. Sadly, Burns died of skin cancer just a year after McDonald's arrival at Celtic, but, as Gordon Strachan's first-team coach, he made a huge impression on the striker from Australia.

"Tommy Burns was amazing," said McDonald. "During pre-season in Switzerland, he pulled me aside a couple of weeks in. He just said to me, 'Block out all of the noise. You're here because you belong here. You're a Celtic player and never forget that. Don't listen to the other stuff. We believe in you and you'll do a great job here'. Coming from him, that was massive because we all know what Tommy means to the club."

While Burns reminded McDonald that there was belief in him inside the club, even if there was a lukewarm reception from some fans, another challenge was to show that he was good enough to compete for a place in the starting XI.

There was intense competition for places up front, from Dutch international Jan Vennegoor of Hesselink, Scotland international Kenny Miller and Polish international Maciej Zurawski, while New Zealand striker Chris Killen had also just arrived.

McDonald's first target was to prove that he was better than some, if not all, of them. It didn't help that he wasn't available for the first match of the season.

"Things started tough as I had to serve a suspension because I was sent off in my final game for Motherwell," he recalled. "I was playing well in pre-season, but a lot of people thought I had gone to Celtic as a squad player. I came back from pre-season hungry and wanting to prove to everyone that I could play at that level. Gordon believed in me, but it was going to be down to my performances.

"Kenny Miller started the first couple of games, though there was talk he was going to leave. He banged in a couple of goals, but he didn't want to play Champions League, so that opened up an opportunity for me. I scored my first goal for the club in the Champions League playoff against Spartak Moscow and never looked back. Scoring that goal on that platform gave me the confidence to kick on. It really helped me settle in. I had done it on the big stage, we qualified for the Champions League, so it felt like I was going to be more accepted and not have to worry about the fan reaction."

That feeling of relief was short-lived. The following weekend, with the score tied at 1-1 at Aberdeen, McDonald failed to find the net and was replaced by Miller, who sealed the win with a late double strike. McDonald was left feeling that he needed to prove himself all over again. The following week, Celtic hit five against Hearts, but McDonald blanked again. Whether or not there was pressure from outside, he was putting pressure on himself.

"In the next game I played, I scored against St Mirren, but I felt I just had to keep proving myself," he said. "The majority of fans accepted me in the end, but there were always a few who just couldn't accept me. I had been at the club two weeks, went to pick up my season tickets, and the woman in the club office abused me because of those goals in 2005. That was the kind of shit I had to put up with, but that was fine. It just spurred me on.

"But despite some negativity, there were great times at Celtic. The people that really mattered—the staff and players—were amazing, and I absolutely loved it. Once I turned things around, the fans were great, and we had some special times.

"I think everyone could see the kind of character I was. I was a guy you loved to hate. I was one of these annoying characters on the field. Off it, I was totally different."

While scoring against Spartak Moscow had helped him settle, a tally of just one league goal in five matches may have seen some question his place in the team. Fortunately, McDonald then hit a rich vein of form. It started with a hat-trick against Dundee United on September 29th. This was quickly followed by his famous winner against AC Milan, before autumn's harvest grew to 12 league goals in eight matches. The tally included a second hat-trick, this time against former club Motherwell.

"It's kind of weird looking back because everything was happening so quickly," said McDonald. "I didn't have time to think. I just did it. I was on the scene and I was hitting really good form at the time. I didn't care who I was playing against. I was at Celtic, I was at Celtic Park. Every time we went out at Celtic Park, I was certain I was going to score—it was just a case of how many. I was playing with all these fantastic players.

"For players who have come from being a big player at a smaller club, how do you go from that to being at a big club with big players and big personalities. How do you cope with that? How do you become what they are? The thing I worked out very quickly, which was maybe something other Celtic strikers didn't, was that I did less for more. I had so many good players around that I just had to focus on doing the simple things well, and get in the right areas, and get on the end of things. That was my biggest asset, and I was clinical."

Even then, nothing could be taken for granted, and Celtic's poor form in December allowed Rangers to gain the upper hand in the title race. Then, back-to-back defeats in early spring saw them going into a league fixture against their rivals four points behind, having played two more games. There was no margin for error. With matches running out, they had to defeat their rivals at Celtic Park to stay in with a chance of winning the league.

April 16th, 2008

After Nakamura puts Celtic ahead with a spectacular first-half strike, Nacho Novo nets an equaliser early in the second half. The game is finely balanced going into the closing stages. A draw suits Rangers, but Celtic need the three points.

With 20 minutes remaining, Nakamura cuts in from the right-hand side of the Rangers penalty area and unleashes a powerful strike that is headed for the top corner of the net. Rangers defender Carlos Cuellar tips the ball over the bar with his hand, conceding a penalty and earning a red card.

Up steps McDonald to take what could be the penalty kick that keeps Celtic in the title race. But Allan McGregor dives low to his left to save, and a golden opportunity is lost.

Into added time, Caldwell receives the ball about 40 yards from the Rangers goal. He swings a cross towards the far post, where McDonald heads the ball back across the six-yard box and Vennegoor of Hesselink dives to nod in the winning goal. The stadium erupts, and McDonald celebrates wildly. His assist has helped to undo the damage done by the missed penalty.

Despite the Champions League heroics and the 21 league goals up until that point, McDonald remains convinced that some fans would have turned on him once again if he hadn't redeemed himself with that late assist.

"I would have been the biggest scapegoat—100%—for what I had done previously," he said. "No matter how many goals I had scored that year, if we hadn't won that game and I missed that penalty, which basically would have meant we had lost the league, where would that have put me?

"So, for about five to 10 minutes, my head was rolling. I had to get myself back in the game, which I did, and managed to do what I did for us to win the game. That was huge. That was one of my biggest moments because it showed real strength of character.

"People couldn't understand what I was thinking at that moment. I had had to do so much to prove myself and for acceptance and it then felt like I could be back to square one in one moment."

There would still be one more huge fixture against Rangers as the Ibrox side started to wobble in the run-in. This time McDonald would emerge as the hero of the hour.

April 27th, 2008

Celtic are now two points ahead of Rangers going into the second home match against them in two weeks. However, they have played three more games, so they need the three points again.

Scott McDonald gives the hosts an early lead, but the visitors turn things around and go 2-1 in front after 30 minutes. McDonald adds his second to level the scores just before half-time.

As in the teams' previous encounter, the game is delicately balanced heading into the final 20 minutes. McDonald runs onto a ball over the top but tumbles under a clumsy challenge from Kirk Broadfoot, and a penalty kick is awarded.

Memories of the miss no doubt still preying on McDonald's mind, Barry Robson takes this one, and fires it down the middle past Neil Alexander in the Rangers goal.

Celtic see out the final 20 minutes. They're now five points clear at the top of the table, though Rangers still have three games in hand.

May 22nd, 2008

Vennegoor of Hesselink heads home the only goal of the game as Celtic defeat Dundee United to lift the title, Rangers having capitulated amid heavy fixture congestion on the home straight. McDonald becomes the fourth Australian to win a Scottish Premier League winner's medal and the second Australian to finish a season as the league's top scorer—his 25 goals matching Mark Viduka's 1999–2000 tally.

From starting the season with doubts over whether or not he would be accepted, and with some expecting him to be a squad player, McDonald ended it as perhaps the most important part of a title-winning squad. He also recognised the importance of the attacking players around him.

"Jan was an amazing partner for me, and an amazing gentleman," said McDonald. "I think we scored about 50 goals between us that season. We were brilliant together. I loved playing with Nakamura as well, and Aiden McGeady was brilliant—a top-class talent. Giving the ball to these two players, you knew you were going to get chances because they were going to make things happen."

Unfortunately, the highs of the first season at Celtic would not be repeated in 2008–09. There were memorable moments, including an excellent strike in a 1–1 draw against Manchester United in the Champions League, and a spectacular effort to defeat Rangers in a crunch match in December.

But the Champions League campaign was hugely disappointing. Having reached the last 16 in the previous two campaigns, the Bhoys went out with a whimper, earning just five points—three of them in a dead rubber at home to Villarreal.

Despite poor form in the Champions League, Celtic went on a 12-match winning streak in the league between September and November. However, in the 22 games that followed, they failed to win more than two games on the spin. They did win the League Cup final with a 2–0 win over Rangers in March, but there was a lack of consistency through the winter and spring months. Despite such patchy form, a 2–1 victory over Dundee United put them in pole position. Wins over Hibs and Hearts in the final two matches would earn them a fourth title in a row. Celtic drew both matches 0–0, and Rangers were champions for the first time since McDonald's late intervention in 2005.

It had the feel of the end of a cycle, and Strachan moved on, meaning big changes were coming. McDonald had again been Celtic's top scorer, netting 19 in the league, but the new manager, Tony Mowbray, seemed unconvinced by his record. Instead of playing to his most effective striker's strengths, he wanted him to play in a less familiar role. McDonald struggled to adapt to Mowbray's demands which, retrospectively, seemed unsuited to some of the personnel he had inherited.

"He didn't really see me as his guy, which was frustrating to say the least," said McDonald. "He spent a lot of money on Marc-Antoine Fortune, so I can understand why he made that call. For me, Tony's ability as a coach was very modern, and possibly ahead of his time. If you look back, a lot of it is bang on the money for how the game is played now. At that time, when I had been top scorer for several years at different clubs, he was trying to change my game for others, and I was thinking 'there's not a lot wrong here'.

"The focal point was around the likes of Shaun Maloney and McGeady. They weren't the goal scorers. For me, the goal scorer still had to get service into the right areas, and Tony was asking me to pull out wide. I didn't understand it, and we had a lot of disagreements."

It seemed that, after just over two years at Celtic, two trophies, and a lot of memorable goals, McDonald's time in Glasgow was already coming to an end. The manager who had effectively ended his time at Southampton before taking him to Celtic wanted another reunion.

"I was in and out of the side a lot," McDonald recalled. "Then I heard Gordon had got the job at Middlesbrough and there were a few offers. It was disappointing as it wasn't working out with the manager [at Celtic] at that point. I could have stuck it out, but Gordon's influence was massive for me as I played my best football under him. He became a real father figure for me, so when the opportunity came to play under him again, I believed we would be successful together.

"And then there was the financial situation as well, and Celtic weren't willing to negotiate. My decision was made, and it wasn't really a tough call because that's the way it materialised. Celtic got their transfer fee, and I had to go. It was quite sad looking back as I went out the back door. But that's football. You can't always have the perfect sendoff. It wasn't the way I wanted to leave. My career should have been a lot longer at Celtic than it was. I was well on my way to 100 goals, which was something I really wanted to achieve. There aren't many that have hit 100 for the club."

It might have been the end of McDonald's time at Celtic, but it was not the end of his adventures in Scotland. Scott spent three years with Middlesbrough before joining Millwall for a couple of years. Having cancelled his contract at Millwall, there would be an unlikely return to his first Scottish club in February 2015.

"Going back to Motherwell was a weird situation for me," he said. "I never planned on being there longer than that first season. Going back to Scotland wasn't really the ambition for me at that point. But it was a win-win for everyone, and it felt right at the time to go and help the club. Motherwell had done a lot for me."

Some strange things had happened in Scottish football while Scott was away. In 2012, Rangers went into administration, with the club ultimately being liquidated. While the name, the colours, the stadium and fan base remained the same, Rangers resurrected as a new company, meaning that the club had to start at the bottom of Scottish football's professional pyramid. Having a budget that dwarfed their lower league competitors, Rangers eased into the second tier with successive promotions, putting them on an unlikely collision course with their old friend and foe, McDonald.

Getting out of the Championship would not prove as straightforward for Rangers as they finished second to Hearts. This meant going head-to-head with Motherwell in a two-legged playoff after McDonald's side had finished second bottom of the Premier League. Rangers were strong favourites, but things didn't turn out as expected, and McDonald couldn't have been happier.

"It was nice to go back there," he said. "When we got out of relegation trouble by winning the playoff, it was an amazing feeling because there were so many jobs on the line for people you knew within the club, including some that had been there for so many years. You went through a lot of emotions because you knew what it meant to others and some of their livelihoods were on the line.

"The Ibrox match was the big one. When I first got there, we were really under pressure to try and reach safety. But we were in decent form at the time, so we were confident going into those two games. With the likes of Lionel Ainsworth and Marvin Johnson, we had real pace.

"I was playing centre-midfield, and not as a striker. I played as a number eight. We took the sting out of the game early on, got the opening goal, and then got another one and another one. It was, like, wow. What's going on here? Then the celebrations at Fir Park were pretty special, and because it was a playoff final win against Rangers, it meant even more.

"It was a massive game because everyone was expecting Rangers to get into the Premier League at that point. We were major underdogs, so it was amazing to win that one.

"The wife and kids were still living in London, so on the long drive home that night, I just had a fantastic feeling, having achieved what we achieved and making sure everyone at the club was safe for another year."

McDonald's second coming at Motherwell was further enhanced by the reunions with some old acquaintances from his previous spell at the club, and from his time at Celtic. He said, "One of the good things about going back to Motherwell was that some former teammates were there—Stephen Pearson, Stephen McManus, James McFadden. It was good fun, and I really enjoyed it. I never envisaged going back the following season, but I changed my way of thinking as I began to see beyond my playing career and wanted to settle my young family.

"We loved living in Scotland and had so many friends there. It was home for us and still is now. When we went back recently on holiday, it was like we had never been away. I started doing media work as well and absolutely loved it. My second time around in Scotland was brilliant."

The same could not be said of his second departure from Motherwell.

"It was great right up until the end," he recalled. "Again, football doesn't always end up the way you want it to. People break promises, and it was a real disappointment that I didn't leave that club on very good terms in the end because of broken promises, which was sour."

With his time at Motherwell over, there was plenty of interest in McDonald, but he would end up at Dundee United—the club where he'd had an unsuccessful trial around 15 years earlier.

"When I had my trial, Ian McCall was the manager, and Owen Coyle was there," said McDonald. "They had a dressing room full of experienced players at that point. Derek McInnes was there, Billy Dodds was there, Jim McIntyre was there. It just wasn't for me. There was no buy-in from the manager. I had just left Southampton and still wanted to be in England. The team went to pre-season in Austria and didn't want to take me, so I wasn't going to wait for them to come back in 10 days' time. It just said to me that they weren't really interested, so I decided to go back down to England."

Dundee United had been among the top sides in Scotland and a formidable force in European football in the 1980s, but they had suffered relegation in 2016. Having failed to win promotion back to the top tier at the first attempt, they turned to the experience of McDonald to help them out.

"It was a bit strange to end up there," he said. "I could have gone back to the Scottish Premiership and played for numerous clubs, but I wanted to go somewhere I could try and win something because they are the special memories and moments that you remember as a player.

"It didn't materialise that way, unfortunately. And manager Ray McKinnon didn't last long enough for it to be enjoyable. I was still living in Glasgow, and new manager Csaba László was expecting me to travel up there five days a week. It was murder. It killed me mentally and made me retire. I hated the travel and what he made us do for the final period. I still don't understand to this day how he got that job.

"It was never going to work in terms of what he wanted to bring to the club. It was just odd—one of the oddest experiences I've had. There were still good times there. I met some good people and good players. I had a successful enough season playing as a striker again and scoring goals. But it was a tough year because expectations at that club are massive.

"It was good to go there as an experience, and the training ground was awesome. But it's hard when you're living in Glasgow and having to travel there every other day. In the end, I decided I wasn't willing to do it anymore."

After that year at Dundee United, it seemed that the curtain was coming down on McDonald's career at the age of 35. Yet there was one more adventure to be had in Scotland. His old Celtic teammate Gary Caldwell was now manager at Partick Thistle and sent out an SOS as a result of the relegation battle his team was involved in.

"Gary Caldwell, who is a really good friend of mine, was badgering me for three or four months to come out of retirement," said McDonald. "I was still training every day on my own, doing a lot of running. But I didn't want to play. I had fallen out of love with it that much because of my time at Dundee United—not so much from a playing perspective, but just some of the people and what was going on around me. I didn't want to be involved in it anymore so that I could be free of being told what to do—it was like being shackled.

"It was lovely to get out of that for five or six months, but there was a carrot being dangled in front of me, and that was going back to Australia and coming out of retirement. I had to prove that I could play again. I got offered the opportunity to move to Australia, but I hadn't played for almost nine months, so clubs didn't know if I was still up to it.

"I had conversations with Gary, and he said that Thistle really needed my help. So I finally agreed, and it was totally different to my recent experiences. Even in my second stint at Motherwell, I felt that I wanted to be at a higher level, so there was sometimes frustration with the environment and the people I was with.

"But I came in at Partick and probably gave a little bit more of myself. I was carefree. I hadn't been involved in the bad results and came in fresh as a daisy and with a spring in my step. I used my experience, and Gary Caldwell just told me to go and do what I needed to do to help the team as a leader.

"I scored on my debut, and I was really emotional. I was interviewed after the match, and I was crying because it was what I had missed, and it had taken me a long time to get back there. I had fallen out of love, but coming back, it felt like it was meant to be. Now I was enjoying it again and doing it for the right reasons, not for money or to get up a ladder. I was just playing to enjoy myself.

"The fans took to me straight away, and I still have a connection to the people there. It's kind of crazy because I only spent three and a half months at the club, but it felt like I had spent three years there—the way I was accepted and the good memories that were made in that short period."

McDonald's time in Scotland started and ended in the relatively humble environments of Fir Park and Firhill, respectively. However, he will always be remembered for the significant contributions he made at all of his clubs. That goal against AC Milan may stand out above all others, but Scott's career in Scotland was about much more than that one incredible moment on a wet Glasgow night in October 2007.

CHAPTER 8
The Standby Socceroo

The road to Kilmarnock began in the sun-drenched beauty of Tuscany after a brief diversion through picturesque Vila Do Conde on Portugal's Atlantic coast.

It was not exactly a conventional route for Danny Invincibile, but he was becoming used to that. He had swapped Sydney for Swindon at the age of 21 as he followed the increasingly well-worn path from Australia to Europe in search of better opportunities than those offered at home.

Invincibile made a name for himself in the Southwest England town as he was their top scorer in his first two seasons and famously struck an injury-time winner against Peterborough in 2001, saving Swindon from relegation.

However, with the club stagnating in England's third tier, the striker began to look elsewhere for his next chapter, and that seemed certain to be in Portugal, until a phone call from Italy changed his career path and life in more ways than he could have possibly imagined.

Invincibile said, "I decided that I needed a different challenge. I was speaking to a lot of other players and some agents.

"I ended up in Portugal with a team called Rio Ave. I had gone there to discuss contracts, and the deal was pretty much done. I went there, spoke to the coach, and took a tour of the ground. I even had a shirt made for me. But there were some nagging concerns about some details that had been added to the contract after terms had been more or less agreed.

"We tried to negotiate for a few days, and then I got a call from Jim Jefferies, who was Kilmarnock's boss at the time. When he had been manager of Hearts, Jim had previously tried to sign me while I was still at Swindon."

While Jefferies had moved on, the Edinburgh club remained interested in the Australian, so there was a lot to consider as Invincibile pondered what was an important career move at the age of 24.

"I also got a call from an agent who wanted to take me to Hearts at the same time. Anyway, I told Jim the situation. I was in Portugal for contract talks, but things weren't going to plan because of the money situation.

"Jim told me that he was in Tuscany for pre-season and invited me to join the squad and train. He said there was no pressure on me. He was happy for me to come and have a look, do some training, and if I felt comfortable, we could have a chat about a few things. But if I wanted to leave, it was no problem whatsoever.

"I thought, fair enough. I went to Tuscany and did pre-season training with Kilmarnock and thoroughly enjoyed it."

While preseason training had convinced him that he might enjoy working with the club from North Ayrshire, there was still some due diligence to be done on whether or not the Scottish Premier League was the right place to be.

He turned to former Swindon teammate and fellow Australian Mark Robertson for advice. Robertson had been at Dundee for a couple of years, so he had the insights that Invincibile needed to convince him to put pen to paper.

"I contacted Mark Robertson, asked him how it was in Scotland, and he was very positive. I think Sky Sports were covering the football at that time, and the league was full of talent and big games, and there was lots of money flowing around.

"One of the most important things for me was to ask about the pitch surfaces, as I was pretty quick and didn't really fancy playing on pitches that were too muddy. Mark reassured me that it would be fine. He only had good things to say about the crowds and the atmosphere. I trusted his opinion, and he turned out to be right.

"Kilmarnock told me they wanted to sign me, though they knew the contract might not be as lucrative as my previous one. But that was it. I went to the boardroom and signed, and that's how I ended up in Kilmarnock in a rather roundabout way."

However, just as Tuscany had captivated the Renaissance artists and the millions of visitors to the region, it was really a short spell in Italy that had convinced Invincibile that his future was in Scotland.

"To be honest, although it was good to hear Mark's views, my decision was made when I was in Tuscany," said Invincibile. "I hadn't been to Scotland before. Perhaps if I had gone to Kilmarnock in December or January, in the middle of some dreich, wet weather, things might have been different. But, as it was, I had been persuaded to join while I was in sunny Tuscany when everyone had smiles on their faces."

It wasn't just about the Tuscan sun and the region's rolling hills and mediaeval architecture, however. Scotland's reputation as a country that was mad about football also had its appeal.

"Of course, I was also well aware of Scotland's pedigree as a footballing country. Everyone knows Celtic, Rangers and Aberdeen, and everyone knows how passionate the people are about the game. Anyone that goes to the stadium for a big game recognises that," he said.

"I didn't know as much about Kilmarnock as the bigger clubs, but I knew that big names like Ally McCoist and Ian Durrant had played there just a couple of years before I joined.

"I looked at how they were doing and the direction they might be taking in the future. For me, it was always more about where the club was at that moment rather than the history. You think about whether or not you're joining a club that's going to be fighting a relegation battle, and they weren't. They were doing quite well in the league, and they seemed to be a stable club.

"Another positive point about Kilmarnock was its location. It wasn't far from Glasgow and Edinburgh, so you weren't isolated in a small town."

An unexpected discovery was that there were also family roots that connected him to the area. "As it turns out, my family tree goes back to Ayrshire on my mum's side—not far from Kilmarnock."

There were a few Aussies in the Scottish game at that time, and some faces were familiar, including Rangers' Craig Moore, who had played with Danny's brother in youth football, and Scott McDonald, who joined Motherwell six months after Invincibile's arrival at Killie.

"When I moved to Scotland, Craig Moore was one of the first people who reached out to me," said Invincibile. "He just let me know that he was there for me if there was anything I needed.

"I knew Scott McDonald from back in Australia. When I was in Scotland at the same time as him and some of the other Aussies, it wasn't like we would hang out together much. When we saw each other, we would have a drink and a chat and a laugh.

"But that was just on the odd occasion. We were a bunch who just got on with it and didn't feel like we had to be with our own. There were meet-ups when I was down in England, and I would catch up with Lucas Neill, Tim Cahill and Hayden Foxe as we were all living around London. In Scotland, we didn't really have those Aussie boy meetups."

It could be said that this was around the time that the trickle of Australians moving into European football became a flood. While the number in Scotland remained modest, all around the continent, Australians were in demand, and Invincibile was part of a very talented crop.

"When I was growing up, in the Australian youth teams, we had the likes of Simon Colosimo, Vince Grella, Mark Bresciano, Lucas Neill, Tim Cahill, Harry Kewell, and Jason Culina. Around the year 2000, we all started to make our way across to Europe, partly because of our own ambitions and partly because the league in Australia at the time was having a few issues.

"Before that time, Aussies had started to move across the world in small numbers, but the best players from my generation all moved because we felt we had to for our careers."

In Scotland, while he saw his fellow countrymen move up a level—as Scott McDonald did when he made the move to Celtic—or move on—as Robertson and Erik Paartalu did after a few years playing at a modest level—Invincibile stayed at the club he grew to love for over seven years.

"Kille were fantastic with me on and off the pitch and I think that's why I stayed so long," he said. "I'm not just talking about the coaching side, but also the club side, including the fans.

"It was a comfortable place, and wherever you went, it was pleasant. At other clubs, there's pressure and the fans are in your face, but there it always seemed to be upbeat and supportive."

At a mid-table club like Kilmarnock, challenging for the league title was never realistic, so the best memories came from playing in big matches, and these experiences remain cherished.

"Scoring at Celtic Park was a highlight given the huge crowd I was up against. Some of my best memories from Kilmarnock are also the cup runs, especially reaching the League Cup final in 2007. At a club like Killie, the league is always out of reach, so the cup runs are always exciting as there are bigger possibilities."

But as well as performing on the park, it was also important to integrate successfully into the squad—not always an easy task for someone who has not been raised in the culture.

"It's fair to say that the UK is very different to the other cultures I have played in," said Invincibile. "I have also played in Australia, Cyprus and Thailand.

"In UK dressing rooms, it's a tough culture. There is a lot of banter, which is a good thing, but you have to make sure you give some back. In Scotland, you can't take things too seriously. You have to be thick-skinned and be able to give it out and take it. And you can't just opt out of it. If you came to training wearing a pink shirt back then, you knew it was getting tied to a lamppost and you were not getting it back.

"If you had a big ego, it would be kept in check. That was one of the biggest things I learned from Scotland. There were no egos, and we were all in it together."

While getting on with teammates was one challenge, another was getting used to the tough treatment from the coaching staff.

"The coaches were hard on us," he said. "If you lost a game and played badly, you were in the dressing room for two hours after the final whistle. You got the hairdryer treatment, and you got pushed around. There was no beating around the bush in Scotland. You had to take it and deal with it."

Despite these features of playing in the Scottish Premier League, Danny did not feel it was a barrier to him or any of the other imports that joined Kilmarnock.

"I don't remember any of the foreign players coming in and struggling to adapt to this. It was more the weather that they had a hard time with.

"In Scotland, the people are generally good fun and friendly and like to have a bit of banter. Although the banter could be harsh at times, it didn't cross a line, and everyone was made to feel welcome.

"Now, I think it's a bit different. Coaches give more specific guidance on what you could do better using data and video clips, and then give you a pat on the back. But back then, that would never happen."

In the mid-2000s, Hibs were noted for producing some of the best young Scottish talents, as the likes of Scott Brown, Steven Whittaker and Gary O'Connor emerged from the Edinburgh club. However, Kilmarnock had two of the brightest prospects, and they would go on to have very successful careers.

"Steven Naismith stood out. He was young when I joined and actually my boot boy. But he was a worker. He just wanted to do extra every day. I also played with Kris Boyd for years, and he was the one that scored all the goals—that was all he did. Both of them went on to do really well in their careers."

However, in terms of pure talent, it was a man from Finland who really stood out.

"In terms of the best footballer I saw there, it was Alexei Eremenko, the

Finnish international. He was phenomenal," said Invincibile.

British football was well known for playing hard off the pitch as well as on it, but the influence of foreign players and coaches had taken hold by the beginning of the millennium. Sports science was highlighting the need for lifestyle changes, and Invincibile was witness to a culture that was in decline, but not altogether disappearing.

"Back then, there was still a drinking culture. It was starting to die down, and there was less of it. You couldn't cut loose at the weekends because there were so many midweek matches. We would normally go out on a Tuesday night because we had Wednesday off if there was no game.

"Nonetheless, there were days when you could smell the alcohol from some of the boys going into training. If you did that now, I don't know what would happen. At that time, the coaches weren't stupid, and they knew what was going on. And the players knew that they had to knuckle down and make sure they worked as hard as everyone else and then some.

"I don't know how some of the Scottish boys did it," he said. "They would put on their training gear and just run. It didn't bother them, and they worked their arses off. There was no feeling sorry for themselves or any signs they were suffering from a hangover.

"The mentality from the coaching staff seemed to be that as long as you did your job, the outside things didn't matter. Unless it was before a game, and then it was a completely different story."

While the off-field antics tended to be led by local lads, imports like Invincibile also got involved, albeit in a more subtle way.

"The Scottish boys didn't really know how to hide it. The foreign players tried to hide their off-field vices and keep things low-key. The Scottish boys would just go out and do what they wanted, and it might get in the press at times. Players do need that time to decompress and have fun, and it's a shame that they can't really do that these days because there is so much scrutiny with social media."

If the regular consumption of alcohol was falling, so was the quality of the Scottish game. The financial excesses of the early 2000s were being replaced by an era of austerity, and that led to an inevitable lowering of standards, as Invincibile recalls: "It changed a lot.

"When I got there, I immediately felt that it was tough. You were playing against the likes of Henrik Larsson, Ronald De Boer and Mikel Arteta. Fabrizio

Ravanelli was playing in Scotland as well. At the time, there was big money, it was a tough league to play in, and the crowds were big.

"There was a real wow factor. But it did change, and it started to decline because of money. It wasn't a sudden change, it happened gradually. The gap between Celtic and Rangers and the rest started to narrow, and it was purely because of the financial situation.

"It was a shame because in the first year I was there, it was just phenomenal. That was because of the standard and everything else about the game off the pitch as well, but the level did go down over the time I was there."

On the subject of standards, the quality of players from Australia had never been higher. The Socceroos had reached the last 16 of the 2006 World Cup and had several players at some of the top clubs in Europe. In the 1980s and 1990s, playing in Scotland's top tier might have been an indication that you were among the top Australian players. By the mid-2000s, however, this was no longer the case.

Invincibile had played for Aussie youth sides and was part of a strong squad at the 1999 FIFA U20 World Cup. Among the future stars at that tournament were Ronaldinho, Roque Santa Cruz, Esteban Cambiasso, Rafael Marquez, Robbie Keane, Ashley Cole, Shinji Ono and Diego Forlan.

Eventual winners Spain had Iker Casillas and a certain Xavi in their side. With the likes of Emerton, Culina, Grella and Bresciano alongside Danny, the Aussies were in good shape and started with a 3-0 victory over Saudi Arabia. Unfortunately, the Mexico of Marquez and Keane's Ireland proved too good, and the young Socceroos went out in the group stages.

As with all youth football, some players went on to have outstanding careers for club and country, others had more modest success, while some failed to make a career from the game. While some of his teammates went on to become mainstays for their country, Invincibile was always just on the outside looking in.

"I lost count of the number of times I was selected on standby for an Australian camp. It seemed to happen most years. Back then, in the competitions, all the overseas-based players would be selected. That meant guys like Mark Viduka, John Aloisi, Emerton, Kewell and all the top stars.

"If there was a smaller tournament held in or near Australia, they would tend to use the locally based players. My recollection is that for the World Cups, almost all of the players selected were based overseas.

"I received a number of letters, maybe around 15, telling me I had been selected in the provisional squad and then nothing. It was almost like getting ghosted.

"I don't look at it as being unlucky. That generation was so good, and I was involved in a lot of the Australia squads below senior level. I got to travel overseas, I went to the U20 World Cup in 1999, and I got to experience big games.

"I just wasn't as good as some of the other players of that generation. Many of them were playing at a higher level. Maybe that was down to me not being as dedicated and pushing as hard as I could have. There are things that all footballers regret, and coaches tell you what you should have achieved, but sometimes it doesn't happen, and it just didn't happen for me.

"I love Australia to bits and I would have been proud to pull the jersey on and have had more of a part in that team. But I'm not bitter about it at all. Those players did so well, and it was great to grow up with that generation and watch them play."

While international football didn't quite happen for Danny Invincibile, he had become a popular figure at his club, staying longer than most players in the modern game. But that seven-and-a-half-year stay was mostly under the guidance of the man who had persuaded him to go to Ayrshire. When Jim Jefferies was approached by his former club Hearts, he couldn't resist returning to the club he loved.

A change in manager meant a change in playing style, and Invincibile was not seen as such a key player any longer.

"Jimmy Calderwood came in when Jim left," he said. "I had known him from years ago, and he had made several attempts to take me to Aberdeen. I almost made the move a couple of times, but for one reason or another, I never ended up signing the contract.

"He had a completely different style from Jim Jefferies. He would come in and tell us, for example, that today we were playing a 4-2-3-1 formation. Then you'd go to training the next week, and he'd tell us we were playing 3-4-3.

"He'd been at Aberdeen for a long time, he knew the players well, and they had got used to his methods. Kenny Shiels was his assistant, and he'd take some of the sessions and want us to adapt to the different formations immediately, and that didn't happen. It had to take time to develop.

"But Jimmy didn't stay for very long, and Mixu Paatelainen came in. He found a system that worked, playing Eremenko and Conor Sammon up front together to get in behind defences. Conor was like a younger version of me. He wasn't very experienced, but he could adapt to certain things that Mixu wanted. Because we were the same kind of player, Mixu basically had to choose one of the two of us, and he preferred the younger player coming through.

"That was pretty much time up for me. I was getting older—over 30 by then—and it was time to move on. The game was evolving. I was quick and strong and direct and powerful, but not the most technically gifted, so the club had to be the right fit for my skill set—this was no longer the case at Kilmarnock."

Invincibile became a free agent at the beginning of 2011, and Perth, Scotland, was his next stop as he signed a short-term deal with St Johnstone.

"I enjoyed St Johnstone because I enjoyed working with Derek McInnes. It's a good club, and Derek was fantastic. I think I was the main reason why things didn't really work out for me there. When you have been at one club for so long and suddenly find yourself out of favour and not getting much game time, you lose fitness, physical strength and confidence.

"So, after getting the move, my attitude should have been to get my head down and work, but there was still a certain sadness about the way things had ended at Killie.

"Derek was very frank with me, and I liked him very much as a person and as a manager. He was pushing me to get the best out of me, but I probably didn't give him my best and work hard enough.

"I had never been told I was surplus to requirements before, so I was at St Johnstone in what was a transition period for me. At the end of that season, I just had to clear my head and make a fresh start."

Invincibile ended his playing career with spells in Cyprus at Ermis Aradippou and in Thailand with Army United. He then stayed on in Thailand as head of the youth academy at Bangkok United, as well as having spells as interim head coach at the club.

At the time of writing, he remains in Thailand with his wife Louise and daughter, but the identity of his spouse made for a somewhat difficult relationship with his old boss at Kilmarnock. Louise's father is Jim Jefferies.

"It's a strange one. I'd never met her for the first few years I was at Killie. And then we made a cup final one year, and everyone brought their families.

"She was there, and I met her. And that was pretty much it for me, if I'm being honest. When we met, we had a chat, we got on well. As soon as I saw her,

I was attracted to her, but I also knew that there couldn't be a relationship out in the open while Jim was my gaffer.

"We stayed in contact for a while, but we didn't really see each other. When Jim left to go back to Hearts, that was when the relationship got more serious, and we could be a bit more open about it.

"At the beginning, it seemed a bad idea, but the feelings grew and grew. It wasn't something that was intended, and I don't recommend it to anyone, ever!

"If anyone knows Jim Jefferies, then you can imagine what I got when he found out about it. But you can't help who you fall in love with. We're still together, and we have a beautiful baby, so that's now about 16 years, so it all worked out in the end."

While falling for the boss's daughter might be unconventional and somewhat stressful, things did eventually become more harmonious. Danny's relationship with Jim is now a warm one; his respect for his now father-in-law has never diminished.

"Other people meet people at work, not so much at football," said Invincibile. "It wasn't easy at the beginning. No one knew about it for a long time, absolutely no one. No players, no staff.

"A lot of people know what Jim is like. He is tough as nails. There's no bullshit. He doesn't take any crap. If he does something, he does it 100 percent, and he wants everyone else to do it properly. He works his arse off.

"He is tough, but he is also one of the nicest people in terms of generosity. If you ask people who have worked with him at the club outside the players, he's generous and kind with them. If a player needed an arm around them, he wouldn't put his arm around them. If a player needed a bollocking, he'd maybe do it times three.

"In terms of our relationship, it may have taken a little while for him to come around and for him to say, alright this is happening. The awkwardness was always on his side because I've always had respect for him, and he'd always been nice to me.

"It probably took a few years for him to accept that it was ok. It's one of those stories that if it gets in the press, it can destroy people's careers. It's one of those scandals that can get out of control if the wrong people find out at the wrong time. But it wasn't like that at all. We're close now. Jim's family."

CHAPTER 9
Adventures in Gretna and Greenock

Just four days after Scott McDonald netted that stunning winner for Celtic against European Champions AC Milan, the striker was again performing late heroics. This time, however, it was in the much more modest surroundings of Fir Park, Motherwell—a place he knew well.

Although the venue was familiar, the Bhoys were not up against McDonald's former club on October 7th, 2007. The opponents were Gretna, the club where fellow Australian Erik Paartalu plied his trade. It would turn out to be McDonald's day, not Paartalu's.

With the promoted club 1-0 up and on the verge of a huge upset against the Scottish champions, New Zealand international Chris Killen levelled the score in the 86th minute, before McDonald's added-time winner.

Paartalu remembers the game well, but for all the wrong reasons: "I was blamed for the defeat at training the next day. I came on as a substitute when we were 1-0 up. The ball went to the left-hand side. I saw Colin McMenamin in the box, and I think I was one-on-one, and Colin was also one-on-one. I thought that if I could whip this in and find him, it could be 2-0 and game over.

"There were just three or four minutes left, plus stoppage time. I should have kept it in the corner. But I whipped it in, it was a shit cross, and it went out of play.

"Celtic then sent the ball long and won a throw-in deep into our half. They took a long throw. There was a guy in front of me, I didn't win the header, and he flicked it onto the far post and Chris Killen scored. And, of course, Scott McDonald went on to score the winner, but he looked offside to me ..."

Paartalu was just 21 years old, and was not too happy to be singled out for blame by Gretna manager Davie Irons after a valiant defeat to the top team in the country at the time.

"When I look back on it, it was such poor management from Davie Irons to hang a young player out to dry," said Paartalu. "At 1–0, you're asking me to do a job that you haven't really been showing me how to do. I couldn't really be blamed for what happened, even though I had a role in it for sure.

"It felt like Davie didn't want to lose the dressing room so he pinned the blame on me. I certainly remember that game as it was a big learning curve. I learned that I had to play even safer, play for time. It's a bad memory."

While Paartalu never managed to reach the career heights of the European-giant-slaying McDonald, his start to life in the UK had some similarities. Erik faced similar challenges in finding a club that would put their faith in him. He was also dependent on funding from his parents for the expenses required to travel across the world as he tried to make his way in the game.

Along the way, he ended up playing a part in one of the more memorable Scottish football stories of the early 21st century.

"The National Soccer League in Australia got shut down when I was 17 and it took 18 months for it to become the A-League," Paartalu recalled. "It went from 13 teams to eight, so for a 17-year-old, it meant opportunities were going to be very limited.

"The change cut out a lot of the younger boys, so I played in the state league for a season. I went for trials with some big clubs in England and Wales, including Watford, Leeds United, Swansea City and Cardiff City. I obviously didn't make it with any of them, but I had stars in my eyes, thinking I was going to get something.

"I returned to Australia and played another half season with a state league team, and that was the year that the A-League started. But I had one last attempt to try and sign with a club in England.

"I was at Doncaster Rovers and thought I was really close to getting a contract, but it didn't happen. The agent that I was working with at the time told me that a club in Scotland needed a defensive midfielder and wanted to have a look at me. The next day, I was on a train to Gretna, which seemed like the middle of nowhere."

Gretna may not have been known to a young Australian trying to make a career in football, but the nearby village of Gretna Green is, according to the gretnagreen.com website, "world-famous as a romantic wedding destination".

You have to go back to the 18th century to learn why. Situated just two miles from the border with England, Gretna Green became the location of choice for young couples seeking to escape the tyranny of disapproving parents. In the words of the same website, "it became a haven for young lovers following the 1754 Marriage Act introduced in England and Wales. You were forbidden to marry without your parents' permission if you were under 21. So the young and in love began eloping to Scotland, where it was much easier to marry".

Paartalu was still under 21 when he rocked up in Gretna in 2006, but his focus was on earning a contract with the local football club—not on getting hitched.

He said, "I had three or four days of training. Straight after the Thursday session, they told me they wanted to sign me in time for the game that weekend. I was surprised it all happened so quickly.

"At that stage, it was just a three-month contract and I was earning peanuts. I was on the bench for the match that weekend. I came on for the second half, hit the crossbar and had a really good debut. The next week, I started against St Johnstone away, and I scored. After that, they offered me a two-and-a-half year extension on double the money, which was still not much.

"That's how it started for me, and it all happened so quickly after it had taken so long for me to get there."

Although Gretna Football Club had not been on Paartalu's radar before he made the trip there to begin a successful trial, the club had been making waves for several years in the Scottish game. Having once been a non-league club in England, they were promoted to the Scottish League's Third Division in 2002. Three years later, they were promoted to Division Two, having won 32 of 36 league matches, and that's where the fun really started.

Gretna had received financial backing from a local millionaire, Brooks Mileson. Key to his vision was the recruitment of seasoned campaigners with Scottish Premier League experience. Their willingness to drop down the leagues gave an indication of the salaries on offer to them, though Paartalu was in no position to bargain for greater riches.

The 2005-06 season demonstrated that Gretna were not your average Second-Division club. They saw off four First Division teams—including the top two of St Mirren and St Johnstone—on their way to a Scottish Cup final appearance against Hearts. The Edinburgh side had finished second in the Premier League that season, but Gretna gave them an almighty scare, taking them to penalties before losing in the shootout.

A significant consolation was the fact that Gretna had won the Division Two title, securing them their second successive promotion. Now, with Paartalu, the aim was to make it three in a row to reach the top of the Scottish football pyramid just five years after starting at the bottom. For Paartalu, however, the aims were more modest. And, for such an apparently ambitious club, so was the infrastructure.

He recalled, "I didn't really care about where I was, I just wanted to play. We didn't have a proper training base, and we had to move all around the country to train. Our stadium had a really low capacity—room for about 3,000 fans. We never trained in the stadium. We had to go to Penrith, which was about an hour away, to use an artificial pitch when it got cold. The other training facility was in Annan, which was also a fair drive from Gretna.

"A lot of the players were travelling down from Glasgow and Edinburgh on a daily basis, bombing down the motorway for two-and-half hours and taking turns driving.

"We had every Wednesday off because it was too much to ask the players to keep coming back and forth. Because the players were so dispersed, every time we had an away game, it felt like a home game for many of the boys because they lived closer to the away grounds than Gretna."

While the club clearly didn't seem set up for the top tier, the rather amateurish organisation seemed to help bond players who had been used to more professional surroundings.

"Despite the challenges, as a group we were really on a roll and had all the ingredients of being a really good team," said Paartalu. "We had a lot of experienced players. And then there was me, a 20-year-old who was just enjoying playing, scoring goals and going out. For me, this was what professional football was all about.

"I was just on a great journey and didn't care about the facilities. I was finally playing regular football for a professional club and enjoying it."

Mileson was often described as charismatic and eccentric. One of his eccentricities was perhaps throwing money at the wage bill rather than the facilities that would help build a sustainable future for the club. But the benefactor knew he was on borrowed time due to long-standing health issues. After his death in 2008, an excerpt from his obituary in *The Independent* read, "As Gretna's owner, he was singularly in control. Players' bonuses included borrowing his Aston Martin for a week. Wages were dished out by personal cheques from him alone. New footballs, and even lunch for Gretna's junior team, were financed from his pocket."

Paartalu never made it into Mileson's inner circle, but he had a good relationship with the man who invested in his dream before time ran out for him and the club.

"Brooks Mileson loved me because I was something different," said the player. "I never got to go to his house, but some of the other lads used to go there and fill their cars up with petrol because he had his own petrol pump. He also had a lot of different animals from various places from all around the world, including alpacas.

"I was this Australian kid, and he wanted to give me a chance. He never really talked to me too much. He was just always there in the background, watching the games.

"I had great respect for him, but I never got to know too much about the financial side. I just knew he had been paying people that should have been playing in the Premier League enough money to persuade them to drop down the divisions. Some of them were getting company cars, free petrol.

"There was definitely more of a relationship between Brooks and some of the older players, whereas I was the shiny new toy who didn't really get involved.

"Even though I didn't get to know him that well, I could see that the people around the club loved him. I remember he got Bobby Robson to come along to a game once."

While the club's journey from obscurity to the Premier League was unconventional, it meant everything to the players who made it happen. Getting over the line was even sweeter as the team wobbled with the First Division title in sight. A run of 10 wins in 12 games between November 2006 and January 2007 had put them in pole position, but they proceeded to win just three of the next 12, squandering what was once a 12-point lead. This left them needing a victory on the final day of the season to earn promotion.

In the most dramatic way imaginable, James Grady clinched the First Division title with a 90th-minute winner to earn three vital points at Ross County.

"Nothing will beat that final day—James Grady getting that last-minute winner to make it 3-2 to seal promotion," Paartalu recalled. "That came after we had really struggled in the final few matches of the season. We just couldn't close it out, and St Johnstone were breathing down our necks. But that winning goal was the pinnacle.

"We had a trip back from Dingwall all the way to Gretna. It is normally a six-hour journey but it took us about 10 as we kept stopping at pubs. It was brilliant.

"You never forget those moments. We had won promotion to the Scottish Premier League and this was in my first season in football. It was just a great feeling to be an Australian kid, playing in Europe after working really hard."

While the wind, rain and slate-grey skies that are common in Scotland are not for everyone, Paartalu embraced the climate, and even those short daylight hours in winter.

"There were some really nice games in the middle of winter," he said. "It was 4pm and it was getting dark, the floodlights are coming on, and you score a header, and then you've got the Christmas night out.

"I was learning so much about the trade. I had so many good men to shelter me and to show me the way. In Australia, we didn't have that culture yet. These were guys like Steven Tosh, James Grady, Allan Main, Chris Innes—a big character who had a lot of time for me—Gavin Skelton and Danny Graham. At some clubs, older players would feel threatened by a younger player coming through, but these guys were all really good with me. All of them were a good bit older than me. When we played together on the pitch, we seemed to know each other inside out, and we also had a great time off it.

"Chris Innes was a real captain—he had a lot of respect from everyone. When tough decisions had to be made, he was the guy that I looked to.

"After my first night out with the team, I was being warned that I couldn't continue like that if I wanted to be a regular in the first team. They taught me a lot about what to do and what not to do. When I look back at my career, there are so many things that I wouldn't have been able to learn in Australia—things like how to see a game out, how to tackle, how not to tackle, how to be aggressive, how to get in people's faces. These were all things I took from Scottish football."

While the 2006-07 season had a dream ending with a third consecutive promotion, the promised land of the Premier League would soon become a nightmare. First of all, Gretna had to move 75 miles from home to host their matches before the money ran out as Mileson's health deteriorated.

Paartalu recalled, "At the start of the season, we had to play all of our games at Motherwell because our stadium didn't meet the necessary standards. Brooks promised the fans that he would put on five or six free buses to take them to the stadium.

"I started to hear about how much it was costing the club for security at Fir Park. If you're playing against teams from the north of the country, like Aberdeen, they're not going to bring 5,000 away fans. So Gretna were paying a lot of money for the security and the usage of the stadium.

"We stopped seeing Brooks at games so often, with the distance to travel probably a factor because his home was so close to the stadium in Gretna."

While there were concerns about the situation off the pitch, Paartalu was finding it more difficult to spend time on it. From being an expected member of the starting XI in the successful promotion campaign, he often found himself out of favour in the first half of the season in the Scottish Premier League.

"During my second season, I was no longer a regular starter, and around Christmas time, I was asked to go on loan to Stirling Albion, who were sitting bottom of the First Division," he said. "At that point, I took it as an insult. However, about two or three weeks after I left for Stirling, I started to hear stories of [Gretna] players who weren't getting paid, or being paid late. Others were having to leave during the transfer window.

"The project collapsed very quickly. It was a real shame. Much of it was down to Brooks' poor health, according to what we were told.

"I had reservations about going to Stirling Albion because it was a step down, and it felt like I was being told that I wasn't good enough to play in the Scottish Premier Division.

"In the end, I think I only played about six or seven games for them, and the travelling was crazy. Because they were part-time, I trained with Gretna Monday morning, Tuesday I travelled from Penrith to Stirling—a two or three-hour drive. I trained there, had Wednesday off, trained Thursday with Gretna in the morning, and then went and did the session Thursday evening in Stirling. I was off on Friday, and then had to drive up for a game on Saturday, so I was getting through the miles.

"Stirling weren't a great side. They were part-time, and you could tell. In some ways, I enjoyed getting away because I felt like I was a good player again, having come from a higher level. But the most significant thing about my time in Stirling is that it led me to go to Morton. My whole life changed there, both on and off the field."

Gretna went into administration, leading to a 10-point deduction that effectively sealed their relegation back to the First Division. But the club resigned from the league as things had completely fallen apart. Mileson was no longer providing the required financial input. He would pass away in November 2008.

Meanwhile, it was time for Paartalu to move on from an interesting adventure that had ended in chaos. He was off to Greenock—a town on the Firth of Clyde, about 30 miles west of Glasgow. It was certainly less isolated than Gretna, but it was known for its past as a centre of industry rather than offering marriage certificates to eloping youngsters.

Just as Greenock's industries had fallen into decline, so had its football team. Between 1964 and 1983, Morton spent just four seasons outside Scotland's top tier. However, from 1983 to 2008, when Paartalu joined, Greenock Morton spent just two seasons in the Premier League, and even had a season in the Third Division.

Near the end of the 2007–08 season in which they had returned to the First Division following a six-year absence, they turned to a young Australian to help them stay there.

"It was ironic because the Morton manager was Davie Irons, who had sent me on loan to Stirling Albion to get rid of me at Gretna," Paartalu recalled. "He needed somebody to play in the number six role for the last five or six games of the season as we tried to avoid relegation.

"I came, we went to Queen of the South and got a 0–0 draw, and I was man of the match, having never met the players beforehand. As things approached the end of the season, we needed to win the final two matches by three goals. We won 3–0 in the second-last match and won 3–0 again at Partick Thistle on the final day.

"In the three years I was with Morton, we always seemed to be battling to avoid relegation until the final few matches of the campaign. It was a hard slog, and we only had one decent season when I was there, finishing sixth or seventh."

There may have been no success to speak of on the pitch, but it was still a hugely significant chapter in Paartalu's development.

"It was a great time in my life, and it was difficult to leave after three years, but I was done and ready to leave. I was 24 at the time. The A-League had been going for a couple of seasons, and had expanded. I wasn't being paid enough money.

"I had a nice off-the-field connection with the town, and the fans. But there were also one or two occasions where I wasn't happy with how I was treated.

"My old Gretna teammate James Grady had come in as the coach, and he left me out for a cup game away to Celtic. I had been struggling with an ankle injury and took an injection to get myself ready. But he left me out of the squad. He had been quoted in the newspapers as saying something like, 'I always talk to my players before the game and let them know if they are playing'. But he hadn't told me.

"I grabbed the newspaper at training, and as he was getting out of his car, I threw it at him and said, 'I thought you were different', and then stormed off to the physio's room.

"The physio told me to go back and sort it out, so I went and spoke to them again and they told me I was out of order. We cleared the air and, after I came back from that injury, I played the house down, so it was good to leave the club after a few good performances.

"I was ready to work back in Australia at that point, but it was a wrench. When I was there, I was taught all about the history of the club. The fans took it seriously and welcomed you in pubs after you had a good game. If you had had a bad game, you were better off staying at home."

Paartalu has fond memories of the Cowshed at Cappielow Park—the section of the stadium that housed Morton's most fearsome fans: "If you were an away supporter, you knew you were going to have a tough day at Morton and, as a player, if you got on the wrong side of the Cowshed, you were going to get dog's abuse. But it was the same in many grounds in Scotland, and you got used to it.

"Because the crowds were relatively small, you could hear lots of the abuse coming from the stands. At first, it makes you more nervous, but it toughens you up. I loved playing there. I loved playing in the cold, when it was snowing, when it was raining. People hated to go there because it was at the other end of the country for a lot of teams."

From his time at Morton, Paartalu recalls the mercurial talents of one particular player. He said, "The best of the lot was probably Peter Weatherson.

"He was an incredible goalscorer and human being but he just couldn't keep his shit together off the field and was always going out. He put on too much weight, but he still managed to play really well. I just wish he had taken care of himself more because he could have been a top player. He was so intelligent with his movement and his goal scoring ability."

While his time in Scottish football was at an end, Paartalu did not dwell too much on the players he had played against but he does recall coming up against one up-and-coming midfielder.

"I didn't pay too much attention to who I was up against and every game away from home was a tough one," he said. "On a good cup run, you were up against difficult opponents.

"We played against Hibs in the cup at Easter Road, and I was up against a young Scott Brown that day. I remember in one moment, he absolutely rinsed us. He got the ball, knocked it between two of us, went around us and made a pass that almost led to a goal. I just couldn't work out how he had taken the two of us out with one touch like that. I always had tremendous respect for him after that, and he went on to have a great career. But even back then, you could tell he was a special player."

Paartalu didn't do too badly either. After leaving Morton, he headed back to Australia, where he played a key role in Ange Postecoglou's Brisbane Roar side as they won the A-League in 2011 and 2012. His form in Brisbane earned him two caps for his country, and he also went on to have spells playing in China, Thailand, Australia (again), South Korea and Qatar.

He wound up his career with Bengaluru in India, where he played alongside Miku—the Venezuelan striker who started for Celtic in their legendary Champions League win over Barcelona in 2012. Paartalu may not be able to boast of having played Champions League football while he was in Scotland, but the journey from failed trials in England to the Indian Super League via Scotland had brought him to the same place as Miku.

CHAPTER 10
The Football Fashionista

"Absolutely nowhere fucking near it. Not even close."

This was Celtic manager Neil Lennon's verdict on Jackson Irvine's first-team debut for Celtic in September 2012. It was revealed by the player himself in an interview on the Open Goal podcast in 2021. Not the most auspicious start for the 19-year-old midfielder, who had been pressed into service due to an injury to Victor Wanyama.

Irvine wasn't the only player to feel the sharp end of Lennon's tongue that day. A defensive mix-up between Mikael Lustig and goalkeeper Fraser Forster had led to Hibernian's second equaliser in a 2–2 draw. Forster bore the main brunt of Lennon's anger, along with the plate of sandwiches that the manager flipped in the dressing room air, landing lettuce and mayonnaise into the hair of some players.

Irvine had joined Celtic as a youth player in December 2010, and impressed enough to become a regular first-team squad member by the beginning of the 2012–13 season. His big moment came in front of almost 46,000 at Celtic Park on September 1st, 2012.

Irvine told Open Goal, "I'd been in most of the squads for the season but hadn't had an opportunity yet. I was on the bench that day.

"It was half-time and Victor Wanyama had hurt his thigh or something like that. I was out warming up … me and Lukasz Zaluska were literally lashing balls at each other at the side of the box, just messing around. I hadn't even brought my jersey out—I'd left it on the bench.

"And then you get the curly finger from the tunnel and you're like, 'oh my god, no way'. The heart starts going at 100 miles an hour. I'm coming on here."

Irvine felt that he did well enough on the pitch, but gifting a goal to Hibs in a match that Celtic had dominated meant that the dressing room would not be a happy place. Two points had been dropped, and Lennon, not exactly the most placid character, was on the warpath.

Irvine, caught in the crossfire that day, recalled, "I was quite pleased with the way it went generally for me. But it was all about results and it was absolute carnage in the dressing room afterwards.

"I got absolutely rinsed. Obviously, emotions are running high after the game, but I'm sitting there, like, 'oh my god'. Every single player got it after that game. It wasn't personal and I recovered from it. I ended up coming back into the (first team) setup the following season. But, yeah, that wasn't a nice moment."

Irvine certainly did recover. Over a decade later, when Australia took to the field against India in their 2023 Asian Cup opener, it is fair to say that the Aussies were looking to Irvine for inspiration. At the age of 30, he had become one of the Socceroos' main men and a veteran of two World Cups.

Irvine duly delivered with the opening goal in a 2-0 victory, and followed up with another goal as Australia defeated Syria 1-0 on Matchday Two. The Socceroos would eventually exit the tournament after an unfortunate loss to South Korea in the quarter-final, but Irvine had made his mark in an Australia shirt once again.

Australia's 2024 squad was not of the vintage variety. The quality was a long way off the golden generation of the 2000s, which featured the likes of Mark Viduka, Tim Cahill, Harry Kewell and Craig Moore.

Irvine was somewhat symbolic of a Socceroos side that is often more than the sum of its parts. The 2022 World Cup side might have lacked the mercurial talent of a Viduka or the pace and skill of Kewell, but in Irvine, they had a very effective team player, and one who started every match in the Aussies' surprise run to the last 16.

While the later stages of Irvine's career have seen him become a key player for Australia and a cult hero at German club St Pauli, the Scottish chapters of his career were challenging at times.

Unlike his hero Mark Viduka, he could not make an impact at Celtic, and that draw against Hibs would turn out to be his only appearance in a competitive match for the first team. Despite having been captain of the U20 side, he was unable to convince either Lennon or his successor, Ronny Deila, that his future lay in the east end of Glasgow.

There seemed to be hope in the summer of 2013 as Irvine started a preseason friendly against a strong Liverpool side. The Hoops won the match 1-0, and

Irvine impressed with his performance, winning the Celtic FC website's man-of-the-match award. He'd held his own against the likes of Steven Gerrard, Philippe Coutinho and Jordan Henderson. However, in his post-match interview with Celtic TV, he acknowledged how hard it would be for him to become a regular fixture in the team:

"I was very happy with my individual performance today, but at the end of the day, I'm looking to get in ahead of guys like Scott Brown, who's obviously the club captain, Joe Ledley—an experienced full international player, who I thought was magnificent today—and there are guys like Charlie (Mulgrew) and Efe (Ambrose), who can also step into the midfield.

"So it's a very hard position to establish yourself in at this club, especially as a young player. It's a tough gig to get a game here. I think maybe going on loan wouldn't be the worst case in the world for me to build up some experience over the next six months to a year, and then bring myself back and hopefully establish myself as a Celtic player."

Irvine would end up going on loan but he would not come back and establish himself. He spent a season at Kilmarnock, where his most memorable moment was a superb long-range strike against future club Ross County. A free kick was rolled across to him from the right wing and, from just outside the D, he side-footed the ball into the top left-hand corner—the perfect blend of power and accuracy. It was the kind of goal that Yaya Toure used to score for Manchester City, and it highlighted the quality Irvine was capable of.

Following his return to Celtic, Irvine had the chance to impress a new manager. Lennon had quit, and Deila was in post. However, rather than a fresh start under a new boss, it was soon to be made clear that there would be no second chance.

"Neil Lennon left at the end of that season and Ronny Deila came in and that was basically the end of me at Celtic," Irvine recalled. "He just wasn't interested. He made it clear to me that I wasn't in his plans at that point."

Another loan move followed, this time to Ross County. The 'Staggies' had ended the 2013–14 season a point above Kilmarnock, the club he had just left. However, their seventh place finish was just five points above 11th spot—the relegation playoff berth—and 59 points behind Celtic in top spot.

It was a very different environment to the one that Irvine had got used to. Ross County is a small club located in Dingwall, a town with a population of approximately 5,500. If moving from the urban sprawl of Glasgow to the Scottish

Highlands was a culture shock, he also arrived at a club in turmoil—manager Derek Adams had been sacked just four games into the season.

The new boss, Jim McIntrye, steadied the ship, and County ended up in a comfortable ninth position to secure their status in the top flight for another year. Irvine's move was made permanent in the summer of 2015, his finest moment in Scottish football ahead of him.

The midfielder really blossomed in his second season at Ross County and the team would make history by lifting their first-ever major trophy. Along the way to the League Cup final, there was the added satisfaction of defeating a Celtic side still managed by Deila.

On that cup run, Irvine also started to demonstrate how much he relished the big occasions. In the quarter-final, his bullet header opened the scoring in the Highland derby against Inverness Caledonian Thistle.

County had what was probably some necessary good fortune in the semi-final, as they played against a Celtic side that went down to 10 men in the 13th minute. A 3-1 comeback win set up a final against Hibs.

At Hampden Park, Irvine played a key role in the opening goal. He seized upon a loose Hibs pass and drove forward before slipping the ball through for Michael Gardyne to net the first goal of the match. Hibs levelled before Alex Schalk's 90th-minute winner earned Ross County the club's first major honour in Scottish football. Irvine was named Man of the Match, and he would soon earn another individual accolade.

After winning the Premiership Player of the Month award for March 2016, Irvine said, "I've come such a long way and I've got everyone at the club to thank. Individual awards only come as a result of you playing in a team, and my teammates have been spectacular this season.

"This club's been pretty fantastic for me. Playing games at this age is so important, and the manager's stuck with me and has always had faith in me, playing me in my natural position as well. It's been a really big step for my development."

Unfortunately for Ross County fans, that development was noticed elsewhere. Burton Albion, in the English Championship, were particularly determined to get their man. The team managed by Nigel Clough had several bids for Irvine rejected before meeting the necessary amount—a club record, thought to be in the region of £330,000.

The *BBC* website quoted County manager Jim McIntrye's reaction: "After refusing a number of bids from Burton Albion, they submitted one that met Irvine's release clause and he has subsequently agreed terms. We reluctantly see Jackson head south."

But it wasn't to be the final chapter in Irvine's relationship with Scotland, five and a half years after his arrival.

Irvine was an immediate hit at Burton, finishing the 2016–17 season as their top scorer and Player of the Year. This impressive form caught the attention of Hull City, and the club from northeast England wanted Irvine to help them back into the Premier League at the first attempt. That ambition would not be achieved, but Irvine quickly established himself at Hull.

He would eventually captain the side during a three-year stay that ended somewhat acrimoniously over the failure to agree an extension to his contract in June 2020. The COVID pandemic was spreading out across the world at the time, making it very difficult to find a suitable new club.

Irvine would be without a club until January 2021, when he returned to Scotland. Irvine announced his move by Tweeting, "I couldn't be happier to have joined @HibernianFC I am over the moon to be back doing what I love and being a part of this great club achieving success!"

It turned out that the deal with Hibs was only for the rest of the 2020–21 season, and it would not be extended. Irvine had returned to Scotland with a bigger reputation, having shone in the English Championship and played in the 2018 World Cup. However, his time at Hibs would be short and somewhat underwhelming.

Patrick McPartlin, editor of the *Hibs Observer*, said, "I don't feel like Hibs saw the best of Jackson Irvine, purely because he hadn't been playing for a while, and maybe wasn't at full capacity when he was a Hibs player, but he certainly added something to the midfield during his short time at the club. He suffered a little from being played out of position on occasion as a result of injuries but you could see his quality."

In the summer of 2021, Irvine signed for St Pauli, and is enjoying a fine spell there as this book goes to print.

However, despite settling in Germany, Irvine's time is Scotland is not forgotten. Indeed, he reminded fans of his roots in the Scottish game when he was on international duty with Australia ahead of the 2022 World Cup. He was seen wearing a classic Celtic shirt, with "Viduka 36" on the back.

After creating a stir on social media, Irvine told *Football Scotland*, "Anybody who knows me or follows my social media knows that I'm a football fashionista. I've always been interested in retro kit and football fashion and culture.

"I've got a big collection at home, and I don't know why I chose to go with that one on the day but I'm glad I did because it got a fair bit of reaction. Duks is one of my heroes, and the fact he wore 36 for Celtic and that was the number I made my debut in [means] it's got a special place in my heart and is definitely one of the favourites on the rack."

Irvine might not have made the same impact at Celtic or, indeed, in English football, as his hero. However, he developed as a player at Kilmarnock and Ross County, which was the springboard to a successful career for clubs and country.

Irvine can even boast of earning more caps and scoring more goals for the Socceroos than Viduka himself. Not bad for the player berated by Neil Lennon as "nowhere fucking near it".

CHAPTER 11
Magic Moments: Tom Rogic

May 27th, 2017—Celtic Vs Aberdeen

Celtic were on the verge of history. The invincible treble was tantalisingly close, but after 91 minutes of struggle at Hampden Park, it was still in the balance.

Brendan Rodgers had been Celtic's manager for a year, and his side had ended a triumphant league campaign unbeaten, and they had also lifted the League Cup, having defeated Aberdeen 3-0 in the final. In the Scottish Cup final, however, the same opponents were proving much tougher to beat.

It was an opportunity for someone to step up and produce what would be the moment of magic that made Celtic the first Scottish club to win the treble of domestic trophies without a single defeat.

That someone would be Tom Rogic.

With 91 minutes and seven seconds on the clock, Rogic picked up the ball 40 yards from goal and immediately accelerated to evade the challenge of Anthony O'Connor. Inside the Aberdeen penalty area, Rogic teased Andrew Considine before making the space to go past him and, suddenly, he was in on goal. The Dons' goalkeeper Joe Lewis was slow in seeing the danger coming, and before he could get his angles right, Rogic had beaten him with a low shot at his near post.

The celebrations were wild, and featured the now iconic image of an overjoyed Rogic pulling at his shirt and basking in the adulation of fans before disappearing under a crowd of bodies.

With an unprecedented achievement on the line, Rogic's late intervention had come on a day when it was unthinkable that Celtic would falter at the final hurdle. After a nervy team performance, Rogic ensured that he would take his place in club history with that moment of inspiration.

That goal against Aberdeen was the crowning glory in a series of moments of inspiration that characterised Rogic's Celtic career. Some of the best examples follow, in chronological order.

March 19th, 2016—Kilmarnock Vs Celtic

After 29 games of a 38-game season, Celtic sat just a point above Aberdeen as the Dons were mounting their most formidable title challenge in a quarter of a century. Not since they took it to the final day of the 1990-91 season had Aberdeen been able to stay in title contention until the home straight.

In February, Aberdeen had beaten Celtic for the second time in that 2015-16 season, suggesting they would not just fold as many observers had expected.

For Celtic, the pressure was on. After a promising first season, manager Ronny Deila was struggling to demonstrate that he was taking the club in the right direction. A disastrous European campaign, an early exit from the League Cup and indifferent league form suggested that, after four consecutive titles, the Scottish champions could be dethroned.

At Rugby Park, Kilmarnock, another lifeless Celtic performance saw them apparently sleepwalking to more dropped points, having drawn two of their previous three matches. It was 0-0 when Rogic replaced Nir Bitton in the 79th minute—Deila turning to the Australian for the inspiration required to keep Aberdeen at a distance and to stay top of the league.

Celtic's title rivals would play later on in the day. If the Bhoys dropped points, a win for Aberdeen would put them on top of the table, albeit having played a game more.

Rogic had been at Celtic for over three years at this point. That period had included a loan spell at Melbourne Victory and then an extended injury absence that saw him miss a whole season in 2014-15. There had been flashes of his potential in 2015-16 but he was yet to convince many supporters that he had a longer-term future at the club. Perceptions really began to change on this day at Rugby Park.

As Celtic's toils continued into the 90th minute, Callum McGregor played the ball inside to Rogic, who was about 30 yards from the opposition goal. The 23-year-old had his back to goal, but he controlled the ball with his right foot and spun away from a tired defender in one quick movement. He took another touch with his left foot to steady himself, and then unleashed a venomous, swerving strike into the top corner.

Deila's celebrations were a mixture of ecstasy and relief. Rogic described the goal as probably the best of his career to date. With one kick, the Australian had swung the momentum of the title race back in Celtic's favour. Aberdeen lost 2–1 at Motherwell later that day and, instead of falling behind, Celtic ended the day four points ahead with a game in hand. Arguably, that one goal had triggered a five-point swing.

Aberdeen imploded, losing five of their final seven matches, and Deila's men cruised to the title, finishing 15 points ahead. Without Rogic's stunning goal at Rugby Park, things just might have been different.

November 27th, 2016—Aberdeen Vs Celtic

Celtic had begun their League Cup campaign in August, and it was a fine Rogic goal that set them on their way to a 5–0 thrashing of Motherwell. The midfielder had made a run into the penalty area when McGregor found him with a chipped pass. Rogic controlled the ball with his right foot and spun around before smashing the ball high into the net with his left peg.

He completed the rout with his second goal of the game in the 76th minute, though this one was a tap-in from a couple of yards out, not the signature spectacular finish fans were becoming used to. Celtic were on their way to the final, reaching it via further wins over Alloa Athletic and Rangers.

Aberdeen were not looking like the team that had pushed Celtic hard the previous season, but they had enjoyed a favourable draw to reach the final.

With Celtic unbeaten in the league and having just been beaten 2–0 by Barcelona in the Champions League (two Lionel Messi goals), the gulf between the two Scottish sides had grown significantly in the nine months since Rogic's spectacular strike at Rugby Park.

Rogic had scored another fine goal in Celtic's 1–0 league victory at Aberdeen in October, and was coming into this match as one of the team's best performers of the season to date. If 2015–16 had been his breakthrough season, in 2016–17 he became one of the players who was expected to make the difference in big matches.

Like Viduka, Rogic's physical build meant that his skill set defied expectations. When we think of playmakers with sublime skills, we often tend to think of somewhat diminutive players like Maradona, Messi, Zico or Roberto Baggio. Or Lubomir Moravcik or Shunsuke Nakamura, to provide a Celtic angle. Even the likes of Michel Platini and Paul McStay were under six foot.

Rogic's tall and slender build gave the impression of an elegant ball-playing centre-back or the type of gangly striker that managers send on to cause chaos as their team chases a late goal. But when you watch Rogic play, you see someone who is blessed with exquisite skills, and they were very much on show in the 2016-17 Scottish League Cup final.

Sixteen minutes into the first cup final of the season, Rogic received the ball on the right wing, cut inside and fired a powerful low shot into the far corner.

Twenty minutes later, he received the ball near the touchline deep inside his own half, facing his own goal. Aberdeen's Graeme Shinnie came across to pressure him. Rogic showed great skill to turn effortlessly inside the defender and leave him trailing. In that situation, most players would have instinctively turned their back on the player that was applying pressure, and perhaps tried to come inside to play safe. But Rogic did the difficult thing—and made it look very easy.

He then drifted forward before finding James Forrest with a pass. Forrest was just inside the centre circle in the Aberdeen half. The winger drove forward and ended his solo run by firing home the second goal.

Rogic had a goal and an assist in his first Hampden final. Moussa Dembele completed the scoring with a second-half penalty, but it was Rogic who had written his name all over this final.

December 3rd, 2016—Motherwell Vs Celtic

Coming into the match, Celtic had dropped just two points out of 39 as Rodgers' side opened up a huge gap at the top of the league table. Motherwell away did not look like the kind of fixture that would threaten that run, but at half-time, a shell-shocked Celtic were 2-0 down, having come into the game on the back of five consecutive clean sheets in the league.

From a Celtic point of view, the game is generally remembered for two things: Kolo Touré's errors and Rogic's dramatic late winner. It was the game that spelled the end of Touré's playing career. The 35-year-old had worked with Rodgers at Liverpool, and it was assumed that he was going to be a squad player rather than a regular starter. However, he was pressed into service and was a regular starter at the beginning of the season before returning players saw him benched.

Erik Sviatchenko's illness saw Touré back in the starting lineup at Fir Park, and he was badly at fault for both of the goals that gave Motherwell their 2-0 lead. A member of manager Arsène Wenger's 2003-04 Arsenal side known as 'The Invincibles', Touré would end the season having played his part in another unbeaten campaign, but this performance was a strong indication that he was no longer good enough at this level.

Fortunately, his teammates would help him out, and Celtic levelled the score at 2-2 in the 70th minute before they almost immediately conceded again to trail 3-2. There was barely enough time to conclude that it was just one of those days when Stuart Armstrong equalised again after a sublime through ball from Patrick Roberts.

Three goals had been scored in three minutes of a breathless encounter, and perhaps both sides would have been ready to settle for a point. A point at home to the champions would be a decent result for the hosts, while Celtic's unbeaten record would be preserved, along with their healthy lead at the top of the league.

Rogic had other ideas. He received the ball about 25 yards from the Motherwell goal, on the left side of the pitch. With a packed defence in front of him, there wasn't much on in terms of passes, so he took matters into his own hands. He stepped into the penalty area, cutting inside the defenders and working the ball onto his right. From about 16 yards out, he found the angle for the shot and fired low into the corner of the net, prompting delirious celebrations.

It was almost a carbon copy of his League Cup final goal, but from the opposite wing. As it turned out, it would not be Rogic's most dramatic late winner of the season.

March 11th, 2018—Rangers Vs Celtic

Rangers had finished a whopping 39 points behind Celtic in the 2016-17 campaign. However, heading into this match at Ibrox, they sat just six points back, albeit having played a game more. Victory would put the Gers within three points of top spot and potentially cause the champions to get a little edgy in the final nine league matches of the season.

If 2016-17 had been a cruise for the Bhoys, 2017-18 was much more of a grind. Brendan Rodgers was having difficult second-season syndrome. Ahead of this clash, he knew that even wins in their final league 10 matches would leave them with 12 points fewer than they had achieved in the previous campaign.

The swagger of the Invincible Treble season could only be seen in occasional flashes as opponents often sat deep and frustrated Rodgers' men. Celtic had been fortunate to take a point in the December clash with Rangers, in which Alfredo Morelos missed several good chances in a 0-0 draw. The Bhoys then dropped five more points before the teams met again, allowing Rangers to close the gap.

But if 2016-17 had been the season in which Rogic had seemed to make things personal any time he played Aberdeen, in 2017-18 it seemed he'd set his sights on Rangers. He had broken the deadlock in September's 2-0 win at Ibrox—one of Celtic's better performances of the season up to that point.

Prior to this fixture, Rangers had won six of their last seven matches, scoring 11 in the previous three. In contrast, Celtic had scored just twice in their last three matches, dropping those five points in the process.

When Josh Windass gave Rangers the lead three minutes into the match on March 11th, it really felt that the momentum was with the Ibrox side.

Step forward Tom Rogic, not long back in the side after a couple of months out with a knee injury.

As Celtic struggled to match Rangers' energetic start in front of a hostile crowd, Rogic picked the ball up in the opponents' half and decided to take it for a walk. From the right side of the pitch, he went inside. He could easily have gone to ground as a poor challenge threatened to end his run early, but he shrugged it off and stayed on his feet.

Rogic was honing in on his target, and the Rangers defence were slow in closing him down. From 25 yards, he unleashed a curling shot with that deadly left foot. It flew high into the net, past the despairing dive of Wes Foderingham.

It was a sensational strike, possibly the best in a crowded field. Finding such placement and power from a distance, while moving across the pitch as a defender was closing him down, was not something many players would be capable of.

The goal came just 11 minutes into a frenetic encounter. It was far from decisive, but it did spark some life into the visitors, and demonstrated that the off-form champions would not go down without a fight. After he scored, Rogic cupped his hand to his ear as the home fans fell silent. The message was clear.

The Gers retook the lead after 26 minutes, but they were pegged back again on the stroke of half-time.

With the score tied at 2-2, Celtic's Jozo Simunovic was red-carded in the 57th minute, resulting in Rogic being replaced as Rodgers sought more defensive solidity. It seemed that the momentum would switch once again, but it was Celtic that found a winning goal through Odsonne Edouard.

It had been a dramatic encounter, and Rogic had been very much in the spotlight with another wonderful goal.

April 15th, 2018—Celtic Vs Rangers

Just over a month had passed since Edouard settled a tight match at Ibrox. The Glasgow rivals would face each other in the Scottish Cup semi-final at Hampden, but this would be nothing like the previous encounter.

At Ibrox, Rangers had pushed Celtic all the way as they battled to stay in with a chance of the title. At Hampden, they failed to lay a glove on them.

Rogic's next magic moment also came in the first half, but this time he was the one to open the scoring and, again, it showed his class.

Celtic had been well on top in the early stages, and it seemed just a matter of time before they opened the scoring. In the 22nd minute, James Forrest found Rogic in a central position, just inside the Rangers penalty area. Ross McCrorie was immediately in his face.

But despite the pressure, Rogic had the skill, strength and balance to perform something of a Cruyff turn to move away from his opponent's attempt to hold on to his shirt. The space had opened up for him to roll the ball into the corner of the net with his weaker right foot from 14 yards out. He lost his balance as he took the shot and fell flat on his back, arms stretched out in celebration.

The Bhoys would go on to win 4-0, setting themselves up to clinch a second consecutive treble in the final against Motherwell.

Rogic still had another goal against Rangers in him, as he netted the fourth in a 5-0 victory in their final league meeting of the season. It was also the game that clinched another title.

September 2nd, 2018—Celtic Vs Rangers

Rangers must have been getting sick of the sight of Rogic at this point. It was a new season and, under Steven Gerrard, the club from Ibrox had ambitions to make a more sustained challenge to Celtic's domestic dominance.

Neither side had started the season particularly well, both having dropped points in their opening three matches, but this was an opportunity for Gerrard's side to lay down a marker, having suffered a couple of heavy defeats to their rivals just five months earlier.

In truth, the gap between the teams looked as wide as ever, but an inspired performance by Allan McGregor in the Rangers goal, with help from the woodwork (three times), had kept Celtic out for an hour. It was time for Rogic to take centre stage once more.

This time, we would not see the Australian score a spectacular goal. Instead, it was all about the surging run he made from just outside his own penalty area to open up the Rangers defence. It was almost literally a box-to-box run and he chose the right moment to release the ball to Edouard, who fed it to Forrest. The winger cut the ball back for Olivier Ntcham to score the only goal of the game.

It was an excellent counter-attacking goal, inspired by the player who just couldn't stop punishing Celtic's biggest rivals.

End of the magic moments?

Just as an ankle injury had kept Rogic out of the squad for a significant part of 2016–17, a knee injury would rob Celtic of his talents for some of 2017–18 and then much of 2018–19.

In early 2019, there was the added complication of his participation in the Asian Cup with Australia. His call-up to the squad caused him to miss a match against Rangers, sparking some lively social media debate, with Chris Sutton at the centre.

The former Blackburn Rovers and Celtic striker turned ubiquitous pundit is never shy of an opinion. He also seemed to relish trolling Aussie fans with lame stereotyping and a condescending attitude to Asian football.

On *BT Sport*, Sutton said, "They don't need Tom Rogic to pump Jordan, absolutely not. It's not right. There are a lot of Scottish football fans thinking the Socceroos should shove their XXXX somewhere the sun doesn't shine. It's not on! It's Mickey Mouse football. Stick to your prawns and your BBQ's, Australia."

While Celtic were losing 1-0 to Rangers at Ibrox, Rogic was with the Australian squad preparing for an Asian Cup warm-up match with Oman the next day. Following a comfortable 5–0 victory for the Socceroos, Sutton couldn't resist taking another swipe on Twitter after Rogic didn't even make the Australian squad: "Well done Socceroos for beating the mighty Oman and leaving Tom Rogic out of the squad ..."

Leaving Sutton's contrived and controversial opinions to one side, the fact that such a storm was created highlighted how important Rogic had become, particularly when it came to the big matches. It was a significant loss for Celtic to have to face Rangers without him, especially considering how much damage he had inflicted on their rivals the previous season.

It didn't help that when he returned from the Asian Cup, Rogic's troublesome knee required surgery.

He was out for a while but did make it back in time to come on as a substitute in a vital late-season clash with Rangers, and he also started the Scottish Cup final against Hearts. By then, there had been a change of manager. Rodgers had left to join Leicester City and Celtic had turned to former boss Neil Lennon to see out the season.

It wasn't pretty at times, but the Bhoys made it an incredible nine trophies out of nine when they lifted the Scottish Cup with a 2–1 victory over Hearts.

Rogic, however, had hit a rough patch. The knee injury had flared up again, causing him to miss the beginning of the 2019–20 campaign under Lennon, who had become the permanent manager.

It wasn't until October 19th that Rogic made his first league start, but he was in and out of the team due to the emergence of Ryan Christie and the arrival of Mohamed Elyounoussi. When Celtic lifted the League Cup with a 1–0 victory over Rangers in December, Rogic was on the bench, while Christie and Elyounoussi started.

The Bhoys won the league title again after pulling away from Rangers in early 2020 before COVID-19 brought an early end to the season. One of Rogic's key contributions was an added-time equaliser at Livingston just before time was called on all sport in March. He had started that game on the bench.

In the final match before lockdown, Rogic provided a sublime assist for Leigh Griffiths in a 5–0 victory over St Mirren that put Celtic 16 points clear of Rangers, albeit having played two games more. It was a reminder of the Australian's rich creative talent, but it had come at the end of another injury-plagued campaign, in which he had not always been first choice.

And then came the COVID season. It was a truly wretched campaign for Celtic as their attempt to make it a record 10 league titles in a row fell flat in spectacular style.

On a personal level, it was another disappointing one for Rogic as he made just 11 starts in the league. He made a substitute appearance when Celtic sealed a quadruple treble by defeating Hearts in the delayed 2019-20 Scottish Cup final, but that was a rare moment of celebration as Celtic relinquished all three titles with a whimper in 2020-21.

Rogic did score a fine goal in the San Siro stadium to give his side a 1-0 lead against AC Milan in the Europa League group stage. Celtic even added a second to lead 2-0 after 14 minutes. But typical of that season, Lennon's side folded, and eventually lost 4-2.

Rogic's career had been drifting somewhat for two years. Things looked a little bleak in the middle of 2021, but salvation was on the way as a familiar face showed up at Celtic Park.

December 5th 2021—Dundee United Vs Celtic

The misery of the 2020-21 season had given way to the optimism engineered by Celtic's new manager—Ange Postecoglou.

The Australian was very familiar with the talents of Rogic, having been the manager of the Socceroos for four years, during which time the Celtic midfielder became a regular in the squad.

Rogic had often been first choice in some of Postecoglou's sides, but there were doubts about the role he might play in a new-look Celtic team. Postecoglou had committed to a major squad overhaul and the implementation of his brand of pressing, attacking football.

While the attacking side was good news for Rogic, the pressing side of his game might have been more of a concern. Rogic was always valued more for what he brought his team in the final third of the pitch than an all-action game.

Fans needn't have worried. Postecoglou recognised his fellow countryman's strengths, and made sure he found a way to use them to his team's advantage, setting Rogic on the way to a memorable farewell season.

He had netted his first goal of the season in a 6-0 thumping of Dundee in August, when Angeball, the general playing philosophy instilled into Celtic by the manager, was beginning to show promising signs, following a tricky start to the campaign.

Rogic had firmly re-established himself in a talented group of players. There was frustration when another injury setback in October forced him to sit out several matches. But he was back at the beginning of December, and ready to paint his final masterpiece.

On a bright, early winter afternoon at Tannadice, Rogic was loitering with intent on the right wing, just inside the Dundee United half. He received the ball and with one touch, took it away from Louis Appéré, who was closing him down. Appéré didn't give up on it—he chased Rogic down the wing, but was shrugged off just as the Celtic midfielder changed direction and cut inside.

Rogic then used his exquisite close control and balance to dance past Adrián Sporle and Ian Harkes and into the Dundee United penalty area. Rogic's former teammate Charlie Mulgrew hesitated as he wondered whether to jockey the run or close down the shot. In the end, he took too long to decide and, as Rogic shaped to shoot, Mulgrew's late lunge landed only after the ball had been curled into the far corner from 14 yards out.

If you could resist any mean-spirited observations on the standard of a defence in the Scottish Premiership, you might enjoy the resemblance to Messi in all but the physical stature of the player involved. The close control, the turns of pace and the mesmerising dribbling were all reminiscent of the Argentinian genius in his heyday.

If there had been any doubt before this strike, it was the most definitive evidence that Rogic was back to his best.

April 3rd, 2022—Rangers Vs Celtic

Rogic's career and his habit of making the difference in games against Celtic's bitter rivals seemed to decline in tandem. Some matches were missed through injury, others he was left out of, and then there were times when he simply didn't have the influence he'd become used to making.

In February 2022, he missed the pivotal 3-0 victory over Rangers due to international commitments. That win had put Celtic top of the league, after the club had trailed by six points earlier in the season.

Days later, Rogic was not only back but turned in a man-of-the-match performance with two fine goals in a 4-0 win at Motherwell.

With seven matches of the season remaining, Celtic led by three points ahead of a game at Ibrox, where they hadn't won in almost three years. On the face of it, a draw might have been satisfactory, but that wasn't necessarily how the visitors saw things.

Rogic's big moment in this game wasn't magical in the conventional sense. It wasn't nearly as brilliant as some of the goals he had conjured up over the years. It wasn't even the decisive goal.

The trick was all about right place at the right time. Just as he had done at the same stadium four years earlier, Rogic struck just as the hosts had begun to smell blood.

Aaron Ramsay's arrival at Rangers that January had made big headlines, but he had failed to live up to high expectations. Three minutes into this match, however, Rangers fans were starting to take to him as he opened the scoring. It was the perfect start for the home side in a match they really needed to win.

Just four minutes later, Rogic silenced the stadium ... again. As Callum McGregor drove at the Rangers defence, Rogic saw his opportunity and moved into the penalty area to offer support to his captain. McGregor found him, and Rogic took one touch before his shot was blocked. The ball ricocheted out to Reo Hatate on the edge of the box, and the Japanese midfielder's low shot was pushed away by Allan McGregor.

That was a gift to Rogic. Still loitering in the box, he was rewarded when the goalkeeper's parry went straight to him. Rogic found the net with ease from just six yards out.

It was only 1–1 and there were still 83 minutes to go, but Celtic's first goal of the match was seen by many as a key moment. Just as Rangers had been threatening to overwhelm their opponents, Celtic showed they were up for the battle—one they eventually won 2–1.

Celtic went six points clear with just six matches left to play and they wouldn't let it slip. It was to be Rogic's final goal for Celtic—and it had been a vital one.

Just under six weeks later, Celtic clinched the title with a point at Tannadice. Two days after that match in Dundee, Celtic confirmed that Rogic would be leaving the club at the end of the season, at the age of just 29—after almost a decade in Glasgow.

He was substituted to a standing ovation as Celtic ended the season in style with a 6–0 thrashing of Motherwell.

Unsurprisingly, Rogic highlighted his magic moment against Aberdeen in May 2017 as a big one when looking back on his career at the club. He told *Celtic TV*, "In terms of moments, the Scottish Cup final one sticks out as one moment, but the number of derby goals and last-minute winners that I can look back on as key moments, I will miss everything.

"I did feel it was important for me to go out on a high and leave as a champion after all the success here. It's another great season to have here.

"It's been a special ride and I've been fortunate to experience so many great memories, at Celtic Park and with the travelling fans."

For the fans who watched him lift 16 trophies in almost 300 appearances, the feeling is surely mutual.

Will Hastie, on signing for Celtic as a 16-year-old, 1989

Tony Vidmar, Rangers, 2000

Danny Invincible for Kilmarnock against Hibernian, 2003

Patrick Kisnorbo for Hearts at Tynecastle Stadium, Edinburgh, 2003

Scott Macdonald on signing for Celtic, 2007

Erik Paartalu for Greenock Morton, 2009

Aaron Mooy for St Mirren during his first stint in Scotland, 2011

Ryan McGowan for Hearts against Rangers, 2011

Jackson Irvine looks at the silverware with Andrew Davies (L) and Alex Schalk (R) for Ross County. They defeated Hibs in the final of the Scottish League Cup, 2016

Martin Boyle celebrates after scoring his second goal for Hibs in a match against Livingston, 2021

CHAPTER 12
Aussies in Leith

"It started off as a joke, and it kind of escalated."

This was how Martin Boyle described the early stages of his international career to *Optus Sport* in 2020.

Boyle's route into the Socceroos setup was rather unconventional given that he had never set foot in Australia when Graham Arnold first expressed an interest in getting him to embrace his father's country.

The winger owes Arnold's interest to the fact that two Socceroos happened to be playing with him at Hibs back in 2018.

In the same *Optus Sport* interview, Boyle said, "I think it was because we also had Jamie Maclaren and Mark Milligan playing for the club. I think I jokingly said my dad was born in Australia and that I was eligible.

"Arnie came in one day at training to see the lads, and he pulled me aside and asked if I wanted to come along to a camp and see how it was.

"I did have to weigh it up (whether to choose Australia over Scotland). I was speaking to my dad, my family, we were having a conversation and then the Scotland manager phoned me as well. By then, Arnie had already asked me to come to camp, and I had agreed, so after that camp I was pretty much committed."

Unlike some other Socceroos in Scotland, Boyle's story did not start with the need to take a long journey across the world in pursuit of a dream. His career did, however, have hardships that were similar to the likes of Scott McDonald and Erik Paartalu.

Boyle started off at Montrose in the fourth tier of the professional game in Scotland. This wasn't even a full-time club, so he had a job doing parcel deliveries while training in the evenings.

Boyle's quality soon stood out and, at the age of 19, Dundee took him to the Premiership and full-time football. But if this was two steps forward, he soon had to take a step back ... all the way back.

Physically, he wasn't ready for the jump and Boyle admitted to *Optus Sport*, "I wasn't built and a bit small, and couldn't really handle the pace, so they loaned me back to Montrose."

Sitting between Dundee and Aberdeen on Scotland's east coast, Montrose does seem an unlikely starting point for a future Socceroo, especially when a player goes to that starting point for a second time.

Even so, the return to the 'Gable Endies' did not discourage Boyle. He buckled down, returned to Dundee and fought his way into the side to become part of a successful promotion campaign in the 2013–14 season.

Boyle was back in the Scottish Premiership, but again, the decision was made that he was not a key part of the team's plans. They let him move on loan to Hibernian for the second half of the season.

Boyle was still just 21, and it must have been disappointing to be shown a lack of belief by the same club twice. Hibs were in the Championship so it meant dropping down a level once more.

He may have been moving down one tier in the Scottish football pyramid, but he was taking a step up in the eyes of the millions of people who consider Edinburgh to be one of the world's most beautiful cities. It has the iconic castle and, just a mile away, the spectacular Arthur's Seat—a hill formed by a long-extinct volcano. The old town is full of character, and then there's the fringe festival, which draws an estimated four million domestic and international visitors to the city each year.

Hibernian's Easter Road stadium is a little bit off the tourist trail, in Leith. The area has undergone some gentrification, but it is perhaps best known as the gritty and often seedy setting for some of Irvine Welsh's best-known novels, including *Trainspotting*. Welsh is one of Hibs' most famous celebrity fans, along with Andy Murray and The Proclaimers. So, yes, Boyle may have been moving down a division, but he was also moving in an upward direction, to Scotland's famous capital city.

Hibs was also a big step up from Montrose. It was one of Scotland's biggest clubs, and Boyle would soon witness one of Scottish football's most memorable occasions this century. Unfortunately, he had to settle for a place on the bench in 2016, when Hibs won the Scottish Cup for the first time in more than 100 years.

After the 3–2 victory in the final over Rangers, the Hibs fans' iconic rendition of 'Sunshine on Leith' went viral, with millions having since viewed it on YouTube. For Boyle, however, it was just the beginning, and Patrick McPartlin, the editor of the *Hibs Observer*, could see why Boyle took time to gain the full trust of the club's managers in the big games.

McPartlin certainly has strong credentials when it comes to evaluating Hibs players, coming from several generations of Hibees supporters, and even one player.

"I was born into a Hibs-supporting family in Edinburgh; our connection with the club started in the late 19th century when my Irish-born great-grandfather arrived in the city and began supporting the team. My great-uncle also played a handful of games at outside-right in the late 1920s."

McPartlin could see the potential in Boyle when he arrived at Easter Road, but he could also see that he still had some way to go in order to become a firm fixture in the first team.

"When he first joined Hibs, he looked raw and inconsistent, with that blistering pace his main selling point," said McPartlin. "He couldn't really be relied upon in front of goal, and he was more a squad player or impact-substitute than a reliable and top-performing starter. But to his credit, he has worked hard season after season to become a key member of the starting XI and the dressing room.

"I feel he sometimes doesn't get enough credit for managing to bounce back from not one but two serious injury lay-offs, and while he might have lost some of his pace with the passage of time, he is still clearly a talented player and, with his seniority at the club, he is someone who will be looked upon as a leader.

"His absence was keenly felt when he left for Saudi Arabia for six months but I don't think many fans would have begrudged him the chance to make a bit more money. There aren't too many characters like him in football these days, and he combines it with doing the business on the pitch as well. He's also not too far off 100 goals for Hibs. Without those injuries, I'm sure he would already have surpassed it—and not many players have managed a ton of goals, so it would be nice for him if he can reach that milestone, such is the service he's given the club."

While Boyle became a very important figure at his club before becoming a regular for his adopted country, he was not the first Socceroo to feature for the Hibees. Almost two decades before Boyle was 'discovered' by Australia, Stuart Lovell was a dependable presence in a fine Hibs team at the turn of the millennium. McPartlin remembers him as an important cog in a team that went from winning promotion to the Premier League in 1999 to finishing third in the top tier in 2001.

"He was signed as an attacker, but more often than not was deployed as a wingback in Alex McLeish's favoured 3-5-2 set-up. I remember him as a hard-working, no-frills player—the type you need in a successful team; a dependable 7/10 most weeks."

Lovell decided to move to Livingston in 2001, and he would again have success. In 2002, Livi finished third in the Premier League in their first season at that level. Then, most memorably, with Lovell as captain, they won their first major honour by beating Hibs in the 2004 League Cup final.

McPartlin does feel that this switching of sides might have had a slight impact on where Hibs fans hold him in their hearts.

"I think he's one of those players who is remembered positively, rather than fondly—captaining the opposition to a surprising League Cup win against Hibs in 2004 didn't go down particularly well in Leith, but he always gave 100% during his time at Hibs and was part of the squad that finished third in 2000–01.

"He also started in the 6–2 victory over Hearts and, like the whole team, performed well on a memorable night for the club. He still occasionally provides co-commentary for Hibs TV, and I think a lot of fans appreciate his insight and analysis—and he's not afraid to tell it like it is, either.

"There were players with whom he shared a dressing room who rightly get more plaudits. Lovell was very much the type of player successful teams need—a player who was perhaps more about graft than skill, but an integral part of McLeish's team."

Though Aussie born and raised, Jamie Maclaren could have been a hero of the Tartan Army rather than a Socceroo. As the son of a Scot, Maclaren was selected for the Scotland U19 side before opting to play for the country of his birth. However, fate would see him make a brief career stop in the country of his father's birth, where his presence eventually drew attention to Boyle.

Maclaren joined Hibs on a six-month loan deal from SV Darmstadt 98 in January 2018 before extending the loan for the full season in 2018–19. While the striker made an excellent start to his time at Hibs, the loan deal was terminated in his second season, allowing him to move to Melbourne City in January 2019.

McPartlin said, "Jamie had a really successful spell at Hibs in the second half of the 2017–18 campaign. He linked up well with Florian Kamberi and Scott

Allan at a time when Hibs were really exciting to watch and had plenty of goals in them. It's just a shame his second stint didn't go to plan; it would have been interesting to see how he fared over the course of an entire season.

"Although I think it was the right move for him to leave for his own career, he was good for Hibs, and I'd have liked for things to have worked out a bit differently for him. Hibs haven't really had a striker in his mould since."

The other player who had a hand in Martin Boyle's call-up goes down as a Socceroos legend: Mark Milligan won 80 caps for his country. His boss at Hibs, manager Paul Heckingbottom, was impressed by his contribution in Scotland.

In a discussion about the departure of former Socceroos skipper Milligan, after the midfieder's final match for Hibs in May 2019, Heckingbottom said, "He couldn't have given any more for the cause. His experience and versatility has been important and Mark's been a great influence on our younger players in particular."

McPartlin was also impressed by the Australian's performances at his club: "Mark Milligan brought a bit of steel into the midfield that had been absent for a while and I'm not entirely sure the players brought in to replace him the following season were able to replicate, or at least cover, what he added in the midfield."

Another Scot who played for Hibs and, surprisingly, became a Socceroo was Jason Cummings. He had long since left Edinburgh when Australia came calling in 2022, but it was in the Scottish capital that he first made his name, from 2013 to 2017, before embarking on a series of moves that arguably resulted in his failure to fulfil his potential.

He had earned a couple of caps in friendlies for Scotland, and the fact that they were friendlies would become important several years later.

A transfer to Nottingham Forest didn't work out, and he went on a series of loans, including one at Rangers, before ending up at Dundee in 2021. His career had a revival of sorts in the east of Scotland. A move to Central Coast Mariners followed, as did a call-up to the country of his mother's birth, and a very unlikely appearance at the 2022 World Cup.

McPartlin has vivid memories of a player who could produce moments of magic, much like Martin Boyle would a few years later.

"I think everyone could see Jason's obvious talent when he was at Hibs—very much one of those players who could conjure something out of nothing, be it a goal from 25 yards or a misjudged Panenka penalty in a cup semi-final!

But, like Boyle, you need characters like Cummings in football, and he could usually be relied upon to contribute in front of goal.

"I suspect he left Hibs a little too early—a season in the Scottish Premiership could well have propelled him to an even higher platform than Nottingham Forest, and I think it's clear that his career dwindled a little at the City Ground, with a couple of slightly underwhelming loan spells before that move to Shrewsbury Town. I think he made the right call in trying to get regular football, and the move back to Scotland with Dundee made sense as well.

"We have seen a lot of players head to the A-League towards the end of their career, so it was a bit of a surprise to see Cummings head out there when he did ... but it turned out to be an inspired move, and credit to Nick Montgomery [Cummings' manager at Central Coast Mariners] and his staff, as well as Cummings himself, for the turnaround in his performances. He had that brief dalliance with the Scotland national team but not to the extent that he ever felt like a long-term option. I also suspect it was partly down to where his career was at the time."

Cummings' improved form was enough to earn him a place on the plane to Qatar for the Socceroos 2022 World Cup finals campaign. The striker's contribution would be limited to a brief substitute appearance in the 4-1 defeat to France in Australia's opening match. However, Cummings still attracted headlines when, after the game, he claimed Kylian Mbappe refused to swap shirts with him and that Olivier Giroud pretended he couldn't speak English.

"In terms of him earning caps for Australia, all I would say is that we learned a long time ago to always expect the unexpected with Cummings," said McPartlin. "He's unpredictable on the pitch and he's unpredictable off it, but there was still something a little bit bizarre about seeing him on the same pitch as Kylian Mbappé, Olivier Giroud, and Antoine Griezmann during the 2022 World Cup. It was entirely unsurprising hearing his comments about trying to swap shirts with Giroud and Mbappé and having no luck, but it was nice to see that he'd retained that mischievous side while reigniting his career."

The Edinburgh derbies nowadays seem to feature as many Australians as Scots, with Hearts having a significant contingent of Aussies as well. But McPartlin does not feel it has added any more sparks to what is already quite an intense rivalry.

"There have obviously been a few Australians on either side of the divide, especially in recent seasons but, if anything, it seems to be more of a friendly rivalry—a group of Aussies in a city thousands of miles from their homeland.

"The rivalry is always there, but it has been brought up a little, particularly with players who were teammates in Australia now being opponents, such as Kye Rowles and Lewis Miller, who were at Central Coast Mariners together. But like most things on Edinburgh derby day, it is a mere subplot in the bigger story."

Lewis Miller's form at right-back resulted in him becoming a full Australian international, while he played alongside midfielder Jimmy Jeggo for a year in Edinburgh. Aussie U23 international Nectarios Triantis joined some of his compatriots at Hibs in a loan deal from Sunderland early in 2024, and he earned his first call-up for the Socceroos squad a year later. Jack Iredale joined the latest group of Australians at Easter Road, and he will aim to make the kind of impact enjoyed by Boyle, Maclaren, Miller, et al.

It was also at Hibs that the Scottish Premiership saw its second Aussie head coach ... sort of.

When Nick Montgomery was appointed as Hibs boss in September 2023, the club's website posted this glowing praise:

"The 41-year-old arrives at Easter Road with a reputation as one of the best young coaches in Australia after leading the Central Coast Mariners to the A-League Championship last season; their first in 10 years."

Montgomery was a Scotland U21 international in an earlier life, but his time in Australia as a player and then manager saw him obtain citizenship, which officially makes him Australian. Unfortunately, despite signing a three-year deal, Montgomery was just another of the coaches in and out of Easter Road's revolving door.

In his brief time in Edinburgh, he did express the view that the club should continue looking for Aussie talent. Montgomery told FTBL, "Aussie players offer good value, and once they get to Europe, their value can sometimes go silly, so it can be a good investment.

"I know that market very well and it's one we're always keeping an eye on. I know Australian players can succeed here in Scotland—that's been proven time and again, and I have no doubt that can continue."

If Edinburgh holds enough attractions to woo millions every year, Leith clearly has something that specifically draws Australian footballers. And it is no different on the other side of the city.

CHAPTER 13
Aussie Blood, Edinburgh Hearts

While Stuart Lovell made the Hibees relatively early adopters of Socceroos in Scotland, it didn't take long for their rivals on the other side of town to catch up.

Gorgie, an area to the west of Edinburgh, is home to Tynecastle Stadium, which was frequently rocking when Craig Levein's side secured back-to-back third-place finishes in 2002–03 and 2003–04. One of the unfortunate features of Scottish football is that being third is as high as most clubs can aim—or at least that's been the case since the mid-1990s, except when Rangers were absent from the top flight between 2012 and 2016.

So third place was quite the achievement for a side that featured Patrick Kisnorbo, who was handed the opportunity to play for Hearts in 2003. He was another Aussie who came with Dave McPherson's seal of approval, and his qualities earned warm praise from a fan turned football journalist.

Many years before Joel Sked became the editor of the *Hearts Standard*, he was a Tynecastle regular who held a season ticket from around the time Kisnorbo joined.

Sked said of Kisnorbo, "He just seemed to fit into the mould of what Hearts were at the time. It was a time when the manager had to cut costs because in the late 1990s and early 2000s, the club spent a lot of money that they couldn't afford.

"Craig Levein came in and he had to cut costs while keeping the team competitive, which he did fantastically well. They came third in back-to-back seasons and Patrick Kisnorbo was part of that team. The team were very physical, they were direct. They knew how to play football, but they could also handle themselves.

"They had a lot of versatile players who you knew would give you 6 or 7/10 every week. There were a lot of players that Levein knew he could trust and ask to do a specific job. And Kisnorbo did that, whether he played centre-back, in the midfield, or you could put him at full-back, and you knew he would do a job. My memories of him are of a reliable presence. He was perfect for Scottish football. In fact, he looked like he was built for Scottish football.

"When you ask fans for their favourite player, Kisnorbo wouldn't fall into that category because of the type of player he was. But he was respected and admired for what he brought to the team to allow others to shine."

Kisnorbo performed so well for Levein that when the manager moved to Leicester City in 2004, he saw him as someone who would be well suited to the English Championship. Kisnorbo decided to join his former boss, and Hearts' first high-profile Aussie was gone in under two years.

Sked said, "Around that time, there were quite a few Australians that came into the youth setup because there was a connection with Dave McPherson. I remember Matthew Park and Rocky Visconte. Visconte was someone who was more memorable because he was a left winger, and he looked quite exciting."

As we saw in the stories of Will Hastie and Lachlan Armstrong, not every young Aussie hopeful managed to make an impact on Scottish football. Hearts offered some a chance, but it didn't work out for a couple of them in the second half of the 2000s, and that might have been something to do with the way the club was being run.

This was the era of the eccentric Lithuanian businessman Vladimir Romanov. His investments boosted a club in financial difficulty in the mid-noughties before leading them into administration almost 10 years later. During his time at the club, he was very trigger happy with managers, and he was not shy about bringing in managers and players from his homeland.

Sked added, "At that time, we had loads of players. Because of our ownership, we had players coming from Lithuania, and there was a massive youth setup. There were always stories about how there would be far too many players at training. It was hard to break into the team, and it was hard to stand out. Without being disrespectful, Matthew Park fell into that category. He never really came through to make a name for himself."

But one of the players who came through the youth system during that period and really did stand out was Ryan McGowan. The midfielder was another who came from the Dave McPherson talent factory, and he did not disappoint.

"Ryan McGowan had the Hearts career that every Hearts fan would want to have," said Sked. "He's not a striker, he doesn't come up with match-winning moments. But he scored against Hibs in a derby win at Easter Road, and he scored in a Scottish Cup final win against Hibs at Hampden Park. So he's done two things that every Hearts fan would give many limbs to be able to do in their lifetimes.

"He also did it in a way [that showed] he got the club. He's now a Hearts fan. It probably helped that he came in early, and came through the academy. When he was coming through the academy, some coaches drummed in the importance of beating Hibs."

The Edinburgh rivalry may not have the worldwide renown of Glasgow's Celtic-Rangers, but for fans in the capital, the derby is more important than any other fixture.

"That's a big thing for Hearts fans," said Sked. "Hearts need to win the derby. Ryan McGowan understood that, even though he came from Australia. It didn't take long for him to get the club, and get what it means to the club. Hearts fans see that and he's still a very popular figure among those fans.

"It was an interesting career just because he was at the club at a very strange time, with the way the club was being run and the way it was headed. But he left a lasting impact, and he probably shouldn't have to buy a drink on Gorgie for the rest of his life."

Unfortunately for Hearts fans, McGowan's form caught the attention of Shandong Luneng in China, and he left for East Asia before his peak years—at 24 years old. One year later, he was starring for Australia at the 2014 World Cup, setting up Tim Cahill for his incredible volley against the Netherlands.

While Ryan earned himself legendary status on the streets of Gorgie, his brother Dylan did not have it quite so good. Like his older sibling, he came through the youth system, but circumstances at the club complicated things and it may have been too much, too soon.

Sked said, "He came through and started playing a lot when the team were in a bad way, so there was a two-year spell where we had to play youngsters because we had a signing ban, and we went into administration, so it was difficult to really stand out in that environment and atmosphere.

"To be a successful player at any club, a variety of things have to go for you, and I just don't think those things went for Dylan.

"Coming through, he was obviously compared to his brother, who was a very popular player amongst the fans, and he came into a struggling team. I don't think, when he did play for the first team, he pulled up any trees or produced any big moments like his brother. There were games when he looked solid, but nothing that indicated that he was going to be there for a long time."

Dylan McGowan recalled the chaos of the period and admitted it made things difficult for him: "The challenges were endless at that time. We had meetings as to which players would get paid and which players would defer till later; we had boys pleading their case to get paid first because they needed it more. It was a really difficult time for the club, points deductions and transfer embargoes aside. It was hard to keep morale high with all that going on."

Despite the inevitable comparisons to his older brother, Dylan very much appreciated his presence at Tynecastle.

"He was a massive help. I think we both helped each other. We lived together and, as you can imagine in a foreign country, leaned on each other a lot."

Although he may not have had the same impact as Ryan, Dylan remains proud of what he achieved at Hearts.

"The highlights were playing in the 2013 League Cup final and winning a lot of the derbies. Overall, playing 70-odd games for a club like that, where you came through the academy, was really special. I think it's an amazing place for the Australians to come and play. I don't think they would have realised how big a football club it is until they arrive here."

A year after Ryan left for China, Dylan returned to Australia to play for Adelaide United, but both would be back in Scotland, though not at Hearts. In what has been a career of many clubs, Ryan was subsequently at Dundee United for a spell before a loan deal at Dundee and late career moves to St Johnstone and Livingston. Factoring in loans at Ayr United and Partick Thistle while a young Hearts player, Ryan has turned out for an impressive seven Scottish clubs. Dylan hasn't travelled quite as much as his older brother, but he has also played for East Fife (on loan), Kilmarnock and Hamilton Academical.

There were plenty of Aussies still to come through the Tynecastle doors, to varying degrees of success. One of them even managed to emulate Ryan McGowan by scoring in a Scottish Cup final. While McGowan's goal came in a 5-1 triumph against Hibs, Ryan Edwards' strike was cancelled out by two Celtic goals in a 2-1 defeat in 2019.

Sked remembers Edwards as much for his energy as his ability. "I remember that Ryan Edwards was regarded as probably the fittest at the club. I remember stories at the time about how well he performed in preseason. There was a time when Craig Levein was manager again and his preseasons were supposed to be really gruelling. Ryan apparently stood out because of his physical capabilities.

"He was a smart pickup by the club because he had done well elsewhere in Scotland. He could come and provide plenty of energy. I think it was at Partick Thistle that he first stood out. He's a player I would have liked to have seen get a good run in the team. He never did.

"Remarkably, he came into the team at the end of the 2018-19 season and scored in the Scottish Cup final against Celtic—a memorable goal that put us ahead. I don't think he got enough of a run or played enough games to allow you to make a proper judgement on him. He went on to have a really interesting career.

"He's gone on to play in Spain and South Korea. He was someone who seemed like quite a sensible signing, but it just never worked for one reason or another. He was a very hard-working guy, which really helps any player coming in at Hearts."

Oliver Bozanic was another Aussie to be picked up by Hearts around this period. In 2018, he made the move from Melbourne City to Edinburgh. Unfortunately, this coincided with a difficult period, despite reaching that 2019 cup final.

"Bozanic played in the team that ended up being bottom when COVID struck," said Sked. "He scored a memorable goal against Hibs, but he wasn't overly memorable for a midfielder."

Ben Garuccio came in at the same time as Bozanic, but, according to Sked, he left an even smaller impression.

"Garuccio was a solid left-back, but he's not going to be someone that's spoken about in Gorgie pubs for years to come."

Despite the modest success of these two players, Hearts have continued to look Down Under for value signings, leading to fans expressing bewilderment at the appearance of more.

Sked said, "There's been a focus on the Australian market for the last few years, certainly under the former sporting director Joe Savage, who took a bit of criticism at the most recent AGM as fans were wondering why Hearts kept signing players from Australia."

And, to put it mildly, results have been hit and miss. "Nathaniel Atkinson came with a good reputation, having won the league in Australia," Sked recalled. "He came as a right-back, which was a problem position. He's had his moments in a Hearts jersey, but he hasn't been consistent enough. Technically, he's quite good.

"Kye Rowles is probably the most interesting one as we saw what he could do at the World Cup in Qatar. He was given a mammoth contract, time wise, because Hearts wanted to protect their asset and get a lot of money for him if he moved on. He has struggled with the physical side of the game.

"He's a really good defender, and I really rate him. If he was to move to somewhere like Italy or somewhere in Europe, I think he'd be a cracking defender because he's great at anticipating where the ball is going to go. He's great at 1:1 duels—we saw that against Kylian Mbappe at the World Cup.

"But there are quite average strikers in Scotland who have got the better of him, simply because they have used their physical ability to rough him up. He's not strong in the air, and in Scotland you need to be strong in the air and stand up to the physical battles. So he can sometimes be inconsistent, depending on which formation we play. He looks better in a back three than in a back four.

"But there's a lot of defensive talent there, and I can see why a lot of bigger teams would look at him and see there's a player there that would suit a league that's not as back to front as Scottish football."

Rowles did eventually decide to try his luck elsewhere, and he crossed the Atlantic Ocean to join MLS side, DC United, in January 2025.

Cammy Devlin may yet be the Australian who is remembered as fondly as Ryan McGowan if the Aussie fatigue that fans have started to experience does not get in the way.

"Cammy Devlin looks like he was made to play in Scottish football," said Sked. "He's really tenacious. He's a wonderful guy, a great character, really popular around the dressing room, and really popular with the fans. But, at the same time, the fans get frustrated with him because they view him as not great with the ball. But winning the ball back, he shows great determination and energy.

"Speaking to people at the club, on the fitness side of things, Cammy Devlin is unbelievable. You can see that in the way he plays. Sometimes, he gets carried away and wants to charge about, close players down and engage with players. He picks up bookings, but I really like his enthusiasm. I think he is a really good player for Scottish football because he's just so in-your-face.

"He has given two of the most memorable individual performances over the past two or three seasons—against Rosenborg and FC Zurich. He just showed the level he could reach. He's been a really popular signing."

However, at the time of writing (early 2025), there remained hope that another player may yet prove to be the best of the lot, despite Calem Nieuwenhof's inauspicious start to life in Edinburgh. Injuries have disrupted his progress, but there have been promising signs.

"For a large part of the start of the 2023-24 season, fans were asking why the hell we had signed this midfielder as he didn't seem to offer anything. But manager Steven Naismith said 'just wait and give him time'. And he then put two to three months together where he was just outstanding—our most consistent midfielder—and he's been a big miss.

"A lot of fans don't realise just how important he is. He does a lot of what Cammy Devlin does, but he does it in a more subtle and controlled way, which I think the manager really likes. There's definitely a player there who could potentially be the best Australian Hearts have signed."

Despite the success of Devlin and the potential of Nieuwenhof, there remains a sense that some fans are growing weary with the recruitment team's focus on Australia.

Sked said, "I've got no real issue where players are signed from as long as they're good players, but there's definitely a feeling that over the last few years, when the team have gone off form, the first thing that fans do is look at the recruitment. And when they look at recruitment, they see that a lot of players are coming from Australia.

"They automatically question why we are continuing to sign players from Australia. It's clearly because there is value for money there, and there are guys who can adapt to the culture in Scotland a lot more quickly, and there's no language barrier.

"So, it's completely understandable why Hearts continue to look closely at this market, but it's certainly treated with disdain when things are not going too well.

"We signed a guy from Colombia and we have signed a couple of guys from Costa Rica. Those guys have a lot more excitement around them, and they'll probably be given a lot more time than players from Australia.

"One of the points made by a fan at a shareholders' meeting was that they

[Australian players] are just all the same. The sporting director highlighted that there was a right-back, a centre-back and a central midfielder. But what the fan was alluding to was that there wasn't a quick guy or an exciting guy or a playmaker. They are guys who are reliable and hardworking."

When many fans thought they were finally getting a player who might have the X-factor that the other Aussie players have lacked, it would be an understatement to say that his time at the club was underwhelming.

It was understandable that there was considerable hype around Garang Kuol, already an Australia international at 18, when Newcastle United signed him in September 2022. Three months later, the striker came close to netting the equalising goal against Argentina when Australia slipped to a 2–1 defeat to the eventual champions in the last 16 of the 2022 World Cup.

When Hearts took Kuol on loan in January 2023, it was seen as quite a coup at a time when the Edinburgh club were in the thick of a battle for third spot. But then the reality of throwing an 18-year-old from the other side of the world in at the deep end began to dawn.

Sked recalled, "I think I referred to him as a wonderkid when I was speaking on the TV once. That was a disappointment. It feels harsh saying that because he was such a young guy coming across the world. He had done well for Central Coast Mariners, but he hadn't played a full season and was not a regular.

"There were mitigating factors at play because he came at a time when Hearts had just gone through a very good period, but then went through a very rough period, during which they lost third spot. He was played in the centre of midfield against Rangers at home alongside another wing-back and an ageing midfielder, Robert Snodgrass, who wasn't the most mobile.

"It was a disaster and it just didn't work. I feel bad for him because there was so much expectation around him, and I think people thought he was going to be this really exciting player who was going to elevate the team—that he was going to come in and make an impact straight away, which, in hindsight, was just unrealistic.

"Scottish football is difficult for anyone to get used to because it's physical and it's really quick. Hearts fans looked at him as someone who had been built up because he went to the World Cup with Australia, and he was coming from Newcastle, so they obviously thought he was going to be good. And when he wasn't, he was completely written off.

"There was a lot of discussion at the time among Hearts fans around the fact that it would have been better to have secured an 18-month loan deal, to give him six months to bed in and adjust, and then you could expect more. Because it was just a six-month loan deal, Hearts fans just wanted him to help the team get over the line and into Europe."

Although Edinburgh has become Scotland's go-to city for Australian football talent, interest from the other side of the globe has perhaps not been reflected in the media coverage.

"I have read stuff in the Australian media from time to time but not so much recently," said Sked. "The Hearts reporter in the *Evening News*—a local paper—wrote a column for an Australian outlet looking at Scottish football because there was such a high number of Australian players in the league.

"I think he was asked to do it because he had a big social media following and there were so many players at Hearts. But it's not the same as with the Japanese players at Celtic, where you go to games and there are Japanese journalists there. There was one game when an Australian media crew came to Tynecastle, but that was just one game."

If Hearts, like neighbours Hibs, live in the shadow of their city's world-famous tourist attractions, they also live in the shadow of the Glasgow giants that dominate Scottish football. However, the Jam Tarts, as Hearts are known, have become a popular club for Socceroos at different stages in their careers.

There has certainly been more of an Aussie presence in the Scottish capital in recent years, with Glasgow having been the city of choice for the early pioneers for the Socceroos in Scotland.

CHAPTER 14
The Late Developer

From St Mirren to Manchester City, via Sydney and Melbourne, Aaron Mooy's route to the top was certainly unconventional. He was not the first player to begin his career in somewhat humble surroundings. However, it was unusual to see an Australian player in Scotland return to his homeland before seeing his career hit new heights in his mid-20s.

Mooy had just turned 20 when he moved to Paisley, having failed to make the breakthrough at Bolton Wanderers, where he had been a youth player since his mid-teens. From the north west of England to the West of Scotland was not a huge geographical shift. Paisley is to Glasgow what Bolton is to Manchester—a town with a rich industrial history that now forms part of the urban sprawl emanating from its much larger neighbour.

Textile production played a big role in the development of both towns, but their football clubs were never among the big hitters of their respective countries. Both had won a few domestic cups but had never been champions, so to reach a higher level, Mooy was very much taking a step sideways rather than a step up.

The midfielder was leaving Bolton as they were reaching the end of the most successful period in their modern history, and he was joining a St Mirren side that had spent the last few seasons flirting with relegation from Scotland's top tier.

If the main reason for leaving the English Premier League was to secure more playing time, it worked. But not to the extent that Aaron might have hoped. He spent much of his first season on the bench, making just seven league starts and coming on as a substitute six times. It might have compared favourably with being limited to the Premier Reserve League North at his previous club, but it wasn't exactly a breakthrough season.

Nonetheless, St Mirren's manager Danny Lennon had seen enough to offer Mooy a two-year extension to the one-year deal he had signed in 2010. He describes how the move came about and some of the challenges the midfielder had.

"We had a scouting network in place, and a club our size was looking at the academies of Premier League clubs. A couple of my good friends, Owen Coyle and Sandy Stewart, were manager and assistant manager at Bolton Wanderers at the time.

"We went down to watch a few games and Aaron Mooy certainly caught the eye for his technical ability. That's what got the ball rolling. We took him for a trial period and really liked him, and we managed to persuade him to join. I spoke to Owen at Bolton, and we managed to strike a deal. I think the fee was only about £50,000 in the end—the only player I actually paid money for in all of my time at St Mirren.

"From when he first came in, he seemed a little bit shy and taken aback by his new surroundings. But he quickly settled and started to win what he needed—an opportunity to be involved in first-team football. Unfortunately, when he joined us, he had a back problem that had to be managed.

"But he made a very positive impression in his first few months, and he seemed to have overcome his injury problems."

Unfortunately, Mooy's second season was blighted by more back problems that kept him out of the side for the first four months of the campaign. He did eventually break into the side when fully fit again, and his most memorable moment in Paisley came in his first league start of the 2011-12 season.

St Mirren were 1-0 down at home to a Rangers side that had been reduced to 10 men when Mooy received a pass on the edge of the opposition box. He danced past a couple of challenges and smashed a left-footed shot in off the post to level the score. It might have looked as if Mooy's career in Scotland was finally ready to take off.

Lennon said, "One of my clearest memories of Aaron was on Christmas Eve 2011. He started the game against Rangers, and we won 2-1. The rain was lashing down, and Aaron scored a fantastic goal—the type of goal we saw on a near daily basis in training. To do that against a top side showed you the potential this boy had."

But the future Socceroo was soon back on the bench for the Buddies, and it was beginning to look like things were not going to work out. Mooy made just three league starts and five substitute appearances in that second season. While he did miss a significant chunk of matches through injury, it was not a sign that he was developing in the way his club had hoped.

Lennon admits that it was perhaps the club's relegation struggles that prevented him from putting more faith in his talented young midfielder.

"Looking back, maybe when Aaron was at St Mirren, a longer run of games would have helped. The first season he was there, we were in a relegation battle, and my judgement was maybe clouded by the fact that I had players who had been in this situation before. We managed to stay up, but Aaron perhaps wasn't getting the amount of game time that his talents deserved.

"I remember when we first had Aaron coming to train with us, we had just signed Paul McGowan from Celtic on a permanent deal. When these two played together in training, they were incredible. They could have kept the ball off the rest of the squad between them. They were excellent at protecting the ball, and they saw things that our other players didn't in their passing.

"Aaron had great potential, and you could see the level he might achieve. My only regret about Aaron is that we didn't get to see more of that ability in a black-and-white shirt due to the fact that he had some injury problems."

Despite the occasional flashes of inspiration and the manager's belief in his ability, it was just one of those moves that would not work in that particular context. Lennon felt it was important to put the interests of the player first.

"He had a very good agent at the time, and I was in regular dialogue with him. His agent wasn't one of those who was just pushing his player's case for starting games or trying to engineer a move to make money. He really cared about Aaron. We spoke, and we wanted what was best for the player.

"In his second season, Aaron was frustrated with the lack of starts he was getting for either tactical reasons or injury problems. He was still under contract, and we certainly weren't trying to push him out of the door. But he was emotionally drained, he was missing home.

"At the end of day, it's only a game of football, and mental health and well-being are more important. We came to an agreement with Aaron and his agent, and Aaron went back to Australia. It didn't surprise me how his career blossomed in more familiar surroundings."

In June 2012, Mooy and St Mirren agreed to part ways. The club's general manager, Brian Caldwell, told the club's website, "This move will give Aaron the opportunity to play more first-team football, which he really needs at this stage of his career. He has been in the UK for the last six years, so I'm sure he will be glad to get back home to Australia, where he will look to push on with his career. We would like to thank Aaron for his efforts while here at St Mirren, and to wish him all the best for the future."

Mooy would return to his home country and join West Sydney Wanderers in the A-League. Aside from that moment of inspiration against Rangers, his time in Paisley was fairly forgettable. With him playing in a league that was not widely followed in Scotland, most fans of the Scottish Premiership would probably not have expected to hear of him again.

Fast forward 10 years, and rumours started to suggest that Mooy was coming back to Scotland. This was a completely different Aaron Mooy. No longer a shy youngster who was struggling to make his way in the game, Aaron was now considered a hugely talented midfield all-rounder capable of playing in many different roles. His creative skills meant that he could be useful as a deep-lying playmaker as well as in a more advanced position, and provide a threat to goal in both roles. He had also earned over 50 caps for his country and had represented them at the 2018 World Cup.

Before his return to Scotland, Mooy had twice been A-League Player of the Year at Melbourne City before a sensational move to Manchester City at the age of 25. St Mirren fans must have been shocked to see the player they let go end up at one of England's top clubs just four years later.

In a move typical of modern football, City immediately loaned Mooy to Huddersfield Town in the Championship. But Mooy's Premier League dream would not be denied, and he played a key role in their promotion to the top tier in 2017. Aaron had two seasons in the Premier League with Huddersfield before joining Brighton.

Given his underwhelming spell at St Mirren, Mooy's career trajectory was a surprise to those who had watched him during his time in Paisley. However, one former Buddies teammate suggested the Socceroo could have done better with more focus.

Hugh Murray told the *Herald Scotland*, "He was very good with both feet, could score goals and pick a pass. He was very talented. At that time, his attitude at times let him down a bit but he was young.

"In training, his ability was clear to see but the other side of the game—his work-rate—was questionable back then. He's improved dramatically in that regard.

"I remember him going back to Australia, but I didn't really follow his career after that. Then one night I was watching a Brighton game and I went 'Jesus, that's Aaron Mooy playing in the Premier League'. It was like watching a different player."

Lennon didn't share Murray's view that Mooy had a questionable work-rate or attitude.

"I don't think that's fair," said Lennon. "Any young player coming in deserves an opportunity to learn from good pros like Hugh Murray. It's up to these individuals to help young players and lead by example. Aaron was coming to a very unfamiliar environment and you could see that at times.

"In Scotland, there's this mentality that everything has to be 100 miles an hour, and during games, you have to be bang at it. Sometimes, I used to analyse Aaron's play during games. You would think that sometimes he could have worked a bit harder to get on the ball.

"But he had a great football brain. When you started working with him, you understood that every other player wants to go to the ball and condense the space, which doesn't give them much time on the ball or space to do anything with it. Aaron was intelligent, and he would let space find him. When you started to understand the way his footballing brain worked, you could see he was a very intelligent footballer.

"When you come to provincial clubs like St Mirren, the Scottish mentality dictates that the one essential condition is that you give your absolute all. I think as a young player, there was a lot of frustration with Aaron because of the stop-start nature of his St Mirren career. It was important that we supported him and tried to develop the potential we knew he had."

Lennon also disagreed with Murray's view that it was a bit of a shock to see Mooy playing in the English Premier League.

"Top managers and coaches see the same things and think they can maximise potential," said Lennon. "Aaron was a player who could handle the ball, had great technical ability and great football intelligence. Other coaches recognised that he had a lot to offer."

One of those coaches happened to be in East Asia, and Mooy's career took an unexpected turn when he left England for China in 2020. In hindsight, Mooy's judgement in joining Shanghai SIPG in the Chinese Super League looks extremely questionable—it happened almost nine months into the COVID-19 pandemic. China's draconian measures ensured that Mooy felt the need to negotiate his release two years later. But it was this release that allowed him to renew his acquaintance with the Scottish Premiership. This time, however, he would not be playing for a team that was battling to beat the drop.

Celtic had just regained the Scottish title from Rangers in 2021-22, under Mooy's former Australia manager Ange Postecoglou. Although he was approaching the age of 32 and had had little game time in several months, Postecoglou was convinced that Mooy had something to offer, even if some fans were not as convinced. Lennon was on the side of the Celtic boss.

"When he came back to Scotland, I watched Aaron very closely," said Lennon. "When you join a big club like Celtic, it's because you've got the credentials to do well and fit into a system. Ange knew him well from managing him for the Australian national team, and to bring him to the club and deploy him as he did was fantastic.

"The media and the Celtic faithful didn't know a great deal about him, so they made things a little difficult. When he arrived, Aaron wasn't completely match fit. I thought that Ange and his staff managed the situation very well, introducing him slowly, coming off the bench.

"You could still see the quality he had in the limited minutes he was getting and fans know good players. Although he was playing deeper, in more of a holding role, Ange saw him as someone the team could build moves through. His decision-making on the ball was key for Celtic at the time. What I loved about seeing him back in Scotland was that he knew how frantic the game could be, but he was always calm and in control of the ball. I think that was what really won over the Celtic fans.

"In the end, he had a great season at Celtic. At one stage, I really thought he was pushing for the Player of the Year awards. From October to January, he played really well."

Indeed, after beginning the season as a squad player who would come on as a second-half substitute, Mooy became a regular starter and formed a formidable midfield partnership alongside Reo Hatate. Despite the plaudits that Mooy ultimately received from the Celtic faithful, Lennon recalled seeing the Australian's discomfort at some of the adulation.

"He was always very humble, even with the success he had at Celtic," said Lennon. "At Celtic, if a substitute has come on and turned a game, or a player has had a particularly good match, they try and get that player to lead the celebrations with the fans, but Aaron was having none of that. He was uncomfortable doing it."

After returning from playing a key role in Australia's 2022 World Cup campaign in Qatar, Mooy seemed to really come into his own for Celtic. In the midst of a purple patch of form, he also became a regular goal scorer. He was outstanding in Celtic's 4–0 win at Hibernian in December, notching a double. In four games from mid-January to early February, he struck four more goals. Perhaps his finest game in a Celtic shirt was in the League Cup final, his passes playing a key role in the build-up to his side's two goals in a 2–1 victory over Rangers.

That was just the first trophy in the treble that Celtic would win that year but, unfortunately, injury problems meant that Mooy missed the run-in, though he did make an appearance as second-half substitute in the title-clinching victory at Hearts.

To the surprise and disappointment of many, this would be the final appearance of his whole career, with Mooy announcing his retirement in June 2023. By this point, Brendan Rodgers had rejoined Celtic as manager, with Postecoglou having left for Tottenham Hotspur.

Rodgers said, "I am delighted for Aaron that he has gone out on a real high after making such a telling contribution to Celtic last season, and that, together with all his other achievements, should be a real source of pride to him."

The manager who first brought Mooy to Scotland had mixed feelings about seeing him hang up his boots.

Lennon said, "I was disappointed when he retired. I enjoyed watching Celtic and the brand of football they played, and it's always good to watch players you have had some influence on in the past. I was enjoying watching Aaron under Ange's system.

"But, like anything, you get to a certain age where you've got to really look at yourself and think about how you want to spend your days in retirement. Aaron served the game well, and he can go and enjoy it. I'm sure he misses the game and still has a lot to offer to the sport, but the most important thing is that he still has his health."

For Mooy, there was great consolation in going out of the game at the top— as a treble winner in the country where he made an inauspicious start, but finished with a flourish.

Mooy told the Celtic website, "I am delighted to finish my career on such a high with Celtic. I was delighted to be part of such a memorable season."

CHAPTER 15
The Boss

Former Scotland international striker turned broadcaster Alan Brazil mocked the arrival of Ange Postecoglou at Celtic on his *Talk Sport* radio show.

First, Brazil, a Celtic fan, made a hash of pronouncing Postecoglou's name, while his sidekick Ally McCoist giggled gleefully. Then Brazil went on to say, "This has got to be a wind-up," and "Where do they come up with these guys?"

McCoist continues to laugh and adds, "I shouldn't wallow in your despair but I'm loving every minute of it".

Talk Sport may be a banter channel that thrives on controversy, but Brazil and McCoist were also speaking for a section of the Celtic support in June 2021. Fan reaction was divided, not helped by the fact that the club had been very publicly rejected by Eddie Howe after a drawn-out courtship.

The media reaction to Postecoglou's appointment was sceptical at best, and disparaging at worst, as Brazil and McCoist demonstrated. In *The Guardian*, Ewan Murray hinted that his age was an issue and that the lack of interest from other European clubs suggested this was a questionable hire, at best.

"He is 55," wrote Murray. "Albeit this continent is not where football starts and ends, it is fair to question why no club of substance in Europe hired him before, especially after guiding Yokohama to league success in 2019. A year later, they were ninth."

In *The Daily Record*, Keith Jackson chose lazy stereotyping and a very crass brand of 'humour' as he quipped, "For all anyone knows at this point, he could be the best thing to come out of Australia since Kylie Minogue's hot-pants."

And this was all before Postecoglou arrived to face a huge rebuild for a side that had finished 25 points adrift Rangers in the 2020–21 season—an outcome that carried the added ignominy of being denied a record 10 league titles in a row. In the 2019–20 campaign, Celtic had reached 80 points after 30 matches and were 13 points ahead of Rangers when the COVID-19 pandemic ended the season prematurely. In 2020-21, the Bhoys managed just 77 points in 38 matches.

Add to this the uncertainty over the futures of several of the squad's best talents, and Postecoglou had his work cut out for him from the first day. The club was, to borrow a popular if somewhat vulgar compound noun, a shit-show.

However, while there was a lot of scepticism, there was also tentative optimism once fans had done their homework and come to understand what their Australian and Japanese counterparts knew. Postecoglou was a talented coach with an impressive CV that included domestic titles in Australia and Japan, an Asian Cup title for his country, and the honour of leading the Socceroos to the 2014 World Cup finals. For good measure, he had also guided his country to the 2018 finals before stepping down ahead of the tournament.

That CV did not seem to carry too much weight on the other side of the world. Plenty of Australian players had made their mark on the Scottish game, but there were still huge doubts about this Aussie coach.

At the time, Hamish Carton was the host of fan media channel *67 Hail Hail*, and Postecolgou's first season at Celtic would inspire him to write the book, *Never Stop: How Ange Postecoglou brought the fire back to Celtic*.

Recalling public opinion in those early days, Carton said, "The first thing that has to be remembered when discussing the appointment of Ange is that it came after months of chat about Eddie Howe becoming the next Celtic manager. Howe was a known quantity from his work in England.

"After the disaster of the COVID season under Neil Lennon, it's fair to say that just about every single Celtic supporter was backing the appointment of Eddie Howe, and it seemed like it was just a matter of time before it was confirmed.

"But, ultimately, the move fell through, for whatever reason. That news came through one Friday afternoon, and within a couple of hours, rumours started circulating that Ange would be the next manager.

"The vast majority of fans in the UK knew nothing about him. While he had managed at a World Cup and an Asian Cup, I can genuinely say that I didn't know the name when I saw it come up. I didn't even have a vague recollection of seeing him at the World Cup.

"To go from assuming we were appointing someone that everyone had heard of to someone that almost no one had heard of was a bit of a shock. There was a period of about 24 to 48 hours when everyone was a bit concerned and frustrated, but that wasn't really about Ange—it was much more to do with the way the club had handled the Eddie Howe talks.

"Then people started to find out more about Ange. Some people we spoke to on our channel knew him from Australia and spoke very positively about him. Everyone that had followed Ange's career seemed to think he was incredible, so you started to believe that this might be a good appointment.

"So after that initial 48-hour period of doubt and frustration, I would say the majority of Celtic fans had a different perspective and started to believe in him.

"You couldn't really get much sense out what was going around in the Scottish media at the time, so you had to look to Australia and Japan to people who knew him. It was important to cut through the noise because so much of it was inaccurate."

Australian football writer Paul Williams, a regular contributor to *The Guardian* and host of *The Asian Game* podcast, was well aware of Ange's abilities, but he was surprised that Celtic would make him their manager.

Williams admitted, "It was a bit of a shock. Everyone in Australia knew the qualities he possessed as a coach, but to break through that barrier and get into European football at a huge club like Celtic almost felt unreachable. When it became apparent that, not only was he on their radar but the move was going to happen, there was a mixture of shock and excitement at the prospect of going to a club with the history they have and the passion of their fans.

"If you go back and look at some of the interactions on social media at the time, there was some scepticism from Celtic fans. There was a level of ignorance because many of them just didn't know who Ange was, and that's understandable because European football exists within a certain bubble, and Ange hadn't penetrated that bubble.

"It reflected a particular attitude within European football, which discounted any achievements that didn't occur within that bubble. When you were reading the reaction on social media, there was a level of frustration that everything he had achieved, including winning the Asian Cup as coach of Australia and winning the league title in Japan—probably the strongest league in Asia—was just discounted as if it didn't matter because it didn't happen in a tournament that was on their radar."

Erik Paartalu, mocked for his take on Ange's arrival, recalls, "I did a couple of interviews with the BBC as he arrived. I was filmed just after coming out of a

COVID quarantine. My quote went along the lines of, the biggest challenge you'll have with Ange is trying to hold onto him after a year or two. And everyone laughed at me.

"While few people in Scotland knew who he was, I knew straight away if he was the way he had been at Brisbane, with Australia and in Japan, he could turn things around. The biggest challenge would be getting the better of Rangers in the league."

So after the initial doubts, there was a level of cautious optimism following some detective work. Then came the actual matches. It might have been reasonable to suggest that things could only get better after a miserable 2020–21 season when fans were absent and performances were sub-standard. However, the start to 2021–22 did not bring immediate relief.

Having finished runners-up to Rangers the previous season, Celtic had to begin their qualification campaign for the UEFA Champions League on July 21st, 2021—just over a month after Postecoglou's appointment.

The first leg of the second qualifying round took place at Celtic Park in front of a sparse crowd due to COVID restrictions. The opponents would be Danish Superliga runners-up, Midtjylland. It was the kind of tie that was seen as tricky but winnable, though context would ensure that it was more complicated than it might have been.

The only new signing available was 19-year-old Israeli winger Liel Abada, who had arrived from Maccabi Petah Tikva. Striker Kyogo Furuhashi and centre-back Carl Starfelt had signed up but could not play due to quarantine requirements. Celtic's best defender Kristoffer Ajer had left for Brentford City in the English Premier League, inspirational club captain Scott Brown had moved to Aberdeen as player-coach, while centre-back Shane Duffy and winger Mohammed Elyounoussi had returned to Brighton and Southampton respectively after the end of their loan deals.

So the squad that had done so poorly the previous season had been weakened. Added to that was the speculation surrounding the future of attacking players Odsonne Edouard—the club's most prized asset—and Ryan Christie. Many fans felt that these two players were as guilty as anyone of letting their standards drop in the previous year, and it had been suggested that their desire to move on was a cause.

Given the importance of the Champions League, the situation was far from ideal. As it turned out, Abada would open the scoring in the first half to raise hopes before his countryman—the experienced Nir Bitton—received a brainless red card on the stroke of half-time to put the pressure back on the home side.

The Danes got a red card of their own 10 minutes into the second half, but it did not shift the game's momentum and Midtjylland levelled the score. A 1-1 draw at home was a poor result but not disastrous. With another week to work with the players, perhaps they would be able to get the result they needed in Denmark.

His side weakened by the absence of the suspended Bitton, Postecoglou chose to change the starting goalkeeper, with Scott Bain replacing Vasilis Barkas for the away leg. The starting back five is considered one of the weakest ever to have taken the field for such an important fixture. You had the second-choice goalkeeper, then a right-back (Anthony Ralston) and an 18-year-old centre-back (Dane Murray), who had both been out of the first-team picture the previous year, and 21-year-old Steven Welsh, who had started to make a breakthrough but was far from a convincing option. Only left-back Greg Taylor had been a first-team regular under Lennon in 2020-21.

In Denmark, Celtic again took the lead through Callum McGregor's stunning volley, but the hosts equalised through Australian international Awer Mabil, and eventually prevailed 2-1 after extra time.

Celtic had failed to qualify for the Champions League for the fourth season in succession and, despite the extenuating circumstances, it was a time for some in the media to suggest that Postecoglou's first big test had been a huge failure.

But this was also a time for the experienced manager to show his skills at dealing with media hyperbole. When a BBC reporter described the defeat in Denmark as a "catastrophic night", Postecolgou responded, "That's pretty strong language, mate. I don't know what your definition of catastrophic is but it certainly doesn't fit my definition of what happened tonight".

When the reporter tried to defend his use of the word, Postecoglou did not give an inch as he said, "Catastrophic to me means the end, and this is far from the end. You're suggesting that this is a club falling apart, and our season's finished. I don't see it that way."

This was an early example of Postecoglou ability to manage the media, and Carton recalls how this had a huge impact on fan perception.

"The way he talks to the media is what gets you on side. He hardly ever gets a word wrong. In his two years at Celtic, I can't remember him saying the wrong things once at a press conference—and that has fans believing.

"An example of the impact he made was when he came out to greet the Celtic Park crowd ahead of that Champions League qualifier against Midtjylland. There were just 9,000 there because of COVID restrictions, but they made him feel very welcome. After doing his pre-match interviews with the TV companies, he got a standing ovation from those that were in the stadium that day. This was before a ball had been kicked competitively."

While the use of emotive language like 'catastrophic' may have rubbed Postecoglou up the wrong way, there was sympathy from Thomas Duncan, writing on the *BBC* website:

"To begin a Champions League qualifying campaign with a centre-back pairing aged 18 and 21, no clear first-choice full-backs or goalkeeper, and a striker in Edouard who clearly sees his future elsewhere is scarcely believable in the eyes of most Celtic fans. And that isn't even the full extent of their problems.

"The club has no head of recruitment, no sporting director and are attempting their largest rebuild in two decades. Postecoglou says he walked into this job with his eyes wide open, and he will largely receive a pass in the circumstances, but with each passing game the scale of the challenge grows."

Three days after the Midtjylland defeat came a loss on Matchday One of the league campaign. Losing 2–1 to a last-minute goal at Hearts was another hammer blow, but at least Celtic could grant Starfelt and Furuhashi their debuts as a new side began to take shape.

Ewan Murray of *The Guardian* was one of those who felt it was time for a dig at Postecoglou, despite the fact that he had been in the job for under two months.

"The 55-year-old, coaxed from Yokohama Marinos via a process which is worthy of scrutiny, is yet to deliver something, anything that infers Celtic have struck coaching gold. Focus on the upper echelons of the club is perfectly valid but the early stages of Postecoglou's tenure are not littered with glimmers of hope. Signing players to suit the style Postecoglou wants to implement—and there is nothing particularly cosmic about that—becomes an increasing struggle as desperation increases."

Hugh Keevins' Opinion piece in the *Sunday Mail* was even less restrained the morning after the loss at Hearts.

"At the very least we now know what the Ange in Ange Postecoglou stands for. Absolutely. Not. Good. Enough."

One game into this domestic season, and Keevins felt the time was right to completely write off Celtic's new boss.

"On the face of it, Celtic offer no challenge whatsoever to Rangers and their visit to Ibrox on August 29 looms on the horizon like a bad accident waiting to happen."

Keevins doubled down by again casting doubt on Postecoglou's credentials, management style and suitability for the Scottish game:

"Ange cuts a detached figure, distant from those around him on the touchline and remote from his players. His post-match comments in Denmark also allowed room for speculation that he doesn't fully understand what he has got himself into at Celtic Park in particular and Scottish football's fevered world in general."

It should be noted that, for the same publication, 23 years previously, Keevins famously described Celtic's signing of the magical playmaker Lubomir Moravcik as follows:

"I don't know what I find more laughable: the fact that Celtic cannot find £500,000 from their biscuit tin to sign a proven talent like John Spencer, or the fact that they then spent £300,000 on one of Dr Jo's (Josef Venglos—Celtic manager at the time) old pals, the unknown Lubomir Moravcik."

Three years later, 36-year-old Moravcik was starring for Celtic in a win over Juventus in the Champions League. Spencer had quit Motherwell to join Colorado Rapids.

So, Keevins may not have been someone to take too seriously for the discerning reader, but as a prominent figure in the Scottish football media, his words carried weight and piled pressure on the Celtic boss.

Relief finally arrived in the following four weeks when Celtic fans got a glimpse of the energetic, free-flowing football promised by their new manager.

First, Czech side Jablonec were beaten 4-2 away in the first leg of the third qualifying round for the Europa League as Furuhashi scored on his first start. Furuhashi then scored a hat trick as Dundee were routed in the league. Jablonec were dismissed 3-0 in the second leg, there was revenge over Hearts in a League Cup tie, while 6-0 was the margin of victory as St Mirren were thrashed at Celtic Park.

Celtic also survived a tight Europa League playoff against AZ Alkmaar, coming through 4-3 on aggregate to ensure group-stage football.

So, things were looking up a month on from a "catastrophic" defeat. But on the horizon were Rangers—the side that had cruised to the title in 2020-21. The Gers had lost at Dundee United on Matchday Two to end a long unbeaten run, but they were still hot favourites to retain their title.

The match at Ibrox on August 29th, 2021, was another big test for Postecoglou and Celtic ultimately came up short in a very tight contest. One goal was enough for Rangers to take the three points but, while disappointing, it was not too disheartening.

Disheartenment was still to come.

After a somewhat unconvincing 3-0 win over Ross County, despite the flattering scoreline, things were to take another turn for the worse.

A 4-3 Europa League defeat at Real Betis may not have been a huge surprise, but Celtic had been 2-0 up after 27 minutes before chaotic defending saw their downfall.

Back in domestic action came a very damaging 1-0 defeat at Livingston. By now, Celtic had strengthened their defence with the addition of Cameron Carter-Vickers and the impressive acquisition of Croatian international right-back Josip Juranovic. Portuguese winger Jota had been signed to add flair in attack.

But in a toothless performance at the memorably named Tony Macaroni Stadium, the new-look Celts slumped to a third league defeat in six matches. The low point of the Postecoglou era came the following week.

A dismal performance saw Celtic draw 1-1 at home to Dundee United and they were jeered off the pitch, ending the match in sixth place in the league, six points behind leaders Rangers after just seven games. This was their worst start to a league campaign in 23 years, and the fan reaction was the first indication that the supporters, having been solidly behind the manager, were beginning to lose patience.

Again, Postecoglou refused to show any signs of panic or dismay, with injuries having an impact on team selection.

"It's quite remarkable that seven games in, people are calling the title already," he said. "It's just not how I work. I'm not pulling up stumps after seven games just because other people seem to think there is some sort of insurmountable challenge out there for us.

"If we weren't playing well, if we were struggling through things, then by all means I would be looking at things a lot differently. With the efforts we are putting in at the moment, and the football we are playing, and the chances we are creating, and what we have got to come back into the team, I just see it totally differently."

A very heavy defeat was to follow but, ironically, it was also when some fans started to see more promising signs of things to come.

A strong Bayer Leverkusen side came to Celtic Park for a Europa League tie, and left as 4-0 winners. But no one would suggest that this was a fair reflection of how the match went. Celtic enjoyed more possession and had as many attempts on goal as their opponents and a similar xG, but the lack of ruthless finishing and defensive slackness gave the scoreline an unfortunate look.

Fans were philosophical, having seen a decent performance, and then came what many now consider one of the most pivotal matches of the season.

After taking an early lead in Aberdeen, the Dons levelled and Celtic were looking at losing more ground in a title race in danger of becoming a procession. Jota came to the rescue, prodding home from close range for a late winner—and things just got better from that moment onwards.

Celtic dropped just four points from the next 15 league matches ahead of a crucial encounter against Rangers at Celtic Park.

Ahead of that, there was a special occasion in December, when Celtic had a League Cup final against Hibs to take care of. It was not a day for the free-flowing football the fans enjoyed, but Celtic dug in, and a double from Furuhashi gave the Bhoys and Postecoglou the first trophy of the season. From a "catastrophic" night in Denmark to trophy winners in the space of five months summed up the rollercoaster of the first half of the season.

Carton insisted that, "Even when we were going through those early season struggles with Postecoglou, there was a feeling that there was something building."

With silverware in the cabinet, Celtic kicked on, and in that February encounter against Rangers, the home side overwhelmed the champions, taking a 3-0 first-half lead with two goals from Reo Hatate, a January signing, and one from Abada.

Celtic were now at the top of the league for the first time that season, and they would not be moved. Carton was now impressed enough to write a book on the experience.

"It was nearing the end of Ange's first season, and we were looking set to win the league. I had seen us win 4-0 against Ross County on the Saturday, and I just happened to be in my local bookstore the following Monday. I was looking at the sports books and, looking at some of the stories, I just felt that season would make a good story given how it had started.

"I then had to learn how to go about writing a book and getting it published.

The timing was not ideal because I had to propose the idea before Celtic had even won the league that season—I think they were four points in front when I submitted my proposal. If they hadn't won the league, there would have been no story.

"But the timeframe I had set out meant that I had to get going, so I started writing, just hoping that Celtic would win the league.

"Fortunately, we did end up winning it, and I then had to think about what would be a logical end point to the book. My deadline was September 2022, and the book would be released in the middle of the next season, so it was a bit complicated."

Celtic would beat Rangers again—at Ibrox—to all but secure the title early in April. This put them six points clear with six matches to play. They dropped just four points in that run of matches and finished off the season with a resounding 6-0 win at home to Motherwell, ending the campaign four points clear of Rangers. It was quite a turnaround after the 25-point deficit of the year before.

The only disappointment in the final stages of the season was losing 2-1 to Rangers after extra time in the Scottish Cup semi-final. But that was quickly forgotten as the title win more than made up for this.

For a man who had been written off by so many and endured such a troubled start, it had been a phenomenal chapter. Winning the league ensured qualification for the group stages of the Champions League, so another chapter lay ahead.

For Williams, his confidence in Ange had been vindicated, and he recalled some of his interactions on social media when Postecoglou was appointed.

"Despite the frustration, there was humour in the social media exchanges because you knew what was coming. You knew that, six months down the line, some of the posts would age very badly, and that's exactly how it turned out.

"It wasn't immediately apparent to the Celtic fans but everyone in Australia knew that Celtic were getting someone special.

"Wherever Ange has gone since he left the national team, media coverage has followed. When he went to Japan, interest in the J.League increased. Scottish football was already big in Australia because of the historical links between the two countries, but Celtic became the adopted team of almost everyone in Australia.

"When you saw the way he quickly won over the Celtic fans, it was immensely satisfying, and there was a huge sense of pride at what he went on to achieve. It was our manager going to one of the biggest and most historic football clubs in the world, with 60,000 fans singing songs in his praise.

"As well as pride, there was also a sense of disbelief at how quickly it happened because, although he had succeeded wherever he went, it had usually taken longer for things to come together. At Yokohama, it took about a year for the team to click but at Celtic it only took a couple of months.

"Watching the wins against Rangers was particularly satisfying. There are many Celtic fans in Australia who grew up with that rivalry, but those who adopted Celtic as their second team under Ange immediately bought into the rivalry and Celtic-Rangers matches became must-watch affairs. They were always early kickoffs in Glasgow, which meant they were shown at a very convenient time in Australia."

There was also a sense of relief in Australia. Had Ange failed to deliver success, Williams feels it could have had a detrimental knock-on effect for other Aussie coaches with aspirations to work at a higher level.

"Everyone in Australian football is invested in Ange because he's almost like a spiritual leader. When he was the national team coach, he was more than just a coach. He was the leader of our game and we were all invested in his journey, so there was an emotional connection with him even if you didn't know him personally.

"You didn't want to see him fail but there was always that 'what if ...' at the back of your mind. We had loudly preached his virtues and abilities. We really wanted him to get to such a big stage, so if he had failed, it could have set back the progress of Australian coaches and made it much harder than it already is to break through. Rightly or wrongly, he was carrying the hopes of an entire country on his shoulders.

"He had to fight hard to find a way back into a job in Australian football after losing his job with the junior national teams. The opportunity only came about when Frank Farina was charged with drink driving and Brisbane Roar needed a new coach. That was a massive sliding-doors moment, and the rest is history."

Paartalu was also pleased to see how his views had been backed up by Ange's achievements: "I love the fact that he was able to turn everyone around in Scottish football. I knew he would. It's infectious when you go and work with him.

"It's strange because I actually had him as Australia U17 coach and he wasn't the same then. I didn't like him at all but I think he was still learning a lot of things.

"Later on, his coaching style was very positive, very vocal and he broke it down so easily. I was particularly impressed by the way he could break it down in a video to make the unimportant people seem important. He would highlight things like the importance of off-the-ball recovery runs. He would highlight how someone had made a great run that went unrewarded. He made everyone aware that if you did something good, he would notice it even if it was the kind of thing that didn't seem that important in the context of the game.

"There were many things with his coaching style that I liked but it was especially about how once you started to understand and play the way he wanted to play, with lots of possession and moving the ball quickly, his confidence made you want to go out and tear it up. It's hard to explain."

Following the failures of the previous year, perhaps the Scottish media had learned a thing or two. Maybe they would recognise that Ange had built a team that would become stronger.

Selected Scottish Premiership predictions for 2022-23

Name	Affiliation	Celtic	Rangers
Kris Boyd	Sky Sports	2nd	1st
Andy Walker	Sky Sports	1st	2nd
Keith Jackson	Daily Record	2nd	1st
Scott Burns	Daily Record	1st	2nd
Robert Grieve	The Sun	2nd	1st
Kenny MacDonald	The Sun	1st	2nd
Hugh Keevins	Sunday Mail	2nd	1st
Andrew Smith	The Scotsman	1st	2nd

Rangers may have lost the league title in 2021-22, but they had reached the Europa League final and brought in a lot of new players. It was no surprise that many of the Scottish journalism establishment fancied them to regain their title.

However, it also felt like Postecoglou was just getting started when Celtic defeated Rangers 4-0 in their first league encounter of 2022-23. This was the sixth victory out of six, opening up a five-point lead in early September. The league would ultimately be won at a canter, sealed with four games to spare in May.

Domestically, Celtic also defeated their great rivals in both cup competitions on their way to a treble. A Furuhashi double won Celtic the League Cup final, while the Bhoys defeated Rangers 1-0 in the Scottish Cup semi-final.

However, while there was domestic dominance, the Champions League campaign exposed the limits of the squad.

Facing European champions Real Madrid on Matchday One with the goal threat of the injured Furuhashi on the bench was not ideal, while loan centre-back Moritz Jenz was pressed into service in the absence of Starfelt.

Despite missing two key players, Celtic attacked Real and for 50 minutes were their equals, coming closest to opening the scoring when Callum McGregor's powerful drive smacked the inside of the post.

But the Spanish side slipped into gear and ran out 3-0 winners at Celtic Park—a stadium that had not witnessed a Champions League match in five years. It was a memorable occasion but a disappointing result.

It was more disappointing to fail to beat Shakhtar Donetsk on Matchday Two when Celtic were by far the better side.

As usual, Postecoglou tried to look on the bright side, but it was very frustrating for the fans to see them claim just a point in a game that they dominated.

The manager said: "More significant than the point was the performance—and the performance was excellent. Obviously, the result was not reflective of that, but they gave everything and that's all I can ask for.

"Obviously we needed that second goal, and we had good chances to get it. We'll get our rewards if we keep playing that kind of football and showing that kind of commitment."

In the Champions League, Celtic didn't keep playing that kind of football, nor did they get their rewards. The campaign petered out with two defeats to Leipzig, a 5-1 thumping in Madrid and another 1-1 draw, this time at home, with Shakhtar.

Postecoglou had answered all the questions required of him in Scottish football, but he was unable to help Celtic punch above their weight in Europe.

His achievements and growing reputation had, however, alerted other clubs and by the end of the 2022–23 league campaign, ominous rumours were spreading about the manager's future. As Celtic prepared for the Scottish Cup final against Inverness Caledonian Thistle, word on the street was that Postecoglou was on his way to Spurs. When offered chances to quash the rumours, Postecoglou was evasive. Days after lifting the Scottish Cup, he was on his way to London.

Inevitably, it was disappointing for Celtic fans who had really hoped to see if Postecoglou might lead them to a bigger impact in Europe the following season.

Carton was philosophical about the departure, preferring to focus on the positives that the Australian had brought to the club. He even got to pass on a copy of his book.

"When it started to become apparent that Ange would be leaving, some fans were in denial," said Carton. "I think most people expected to get at least a third year out of him, so it came as a bit of a shock. Looking back, we were maybe a bit unlucky that Spurs targeted him.

"On the final day of the 2022–23 league season, after the presentation of the championship trophy, I finally met him. We had been doing some video work and were packing our stuff away, and about to head home when he shouted me over and told me that he loved my book."

His wife was also there and she did a lot of the talking. She told me she was reading the book and was loving it.

"It was great to meet him one-on-one and shake his hand. I thanked him for what he had done for the club because there was a feeling at that stage that he may move on.

"There was a day I had wanted to personally give Ange a copy of my book, just after it had come out. I was going to be attending the post-match press conference, so it seemed the perfect opportunity.

"I arranged it through Ian Jamieson, a friend who works in the PR department at the club. Unfortunately, this presentation of the book was based on the assumption that we would beat Motherwell at home that day in April.

"We played poorly and drew 1–1, so it was suggested that Ange was not in the right mood to be presented with a book. It wasn't that he didn't want the book, but just that it wasn't the right day for it.

"I left the copy of the book with Ian, but felt that it would probably never make it onto Ange's desk. But Ian made sure that Ange received the book and when we met, he made it clear that he knew I had written it and his wife was reading it.

"As time goes on, I hope that in the years to come, the book will still have a shelf life as a reminder of what was a special season.

"In his whole career, Ange has always looked to reach the top of football and, harsh as it sounds, Celtic were never more than a step on that journey. I'm not suggesting that Ange had that in mind when he was at the club as he had to do well in order to get that next move.

"He wasn't a Celtic fan. He never claimed to be a Celtic fan. He came in to do a job, and he did it brilliantly, so it's hard to complain. As time goes on, everyone will look back and appreciate what a good two years he had."

In a two-year term, Ange Postecoglou had achieved an incredible turnaround from the lows of July 2021. An "unknown" from Australia had proven many doubters wrong by quickly wrestling domestic supremacy back from Rangers.

However, Carton agrees that he did not have the longevity to be considered a Celtic legend, and nor did he have the success in Europe to be as successful as Martin O'Neill or Gordon Strachan.

"In terms of his legacy, there were times when people were comparing him to Jock Stein, a comparison that hasn't aged well given he only stayed for two years. It was a really short chapter in his career. But domestically, he was as good as anyone.

"In that first season, winning two trophies and winning the league ahead of a Rangers team that reached the Europa League final was a great achievement. In the second season, to win a treble by beating Rangers in every competition was another big achievement.

"But the European record doesn't stack up well, even against other managers from the 21st century, like Martin O'Neill and Gordon Strachan.

"It was an incredible two years, nonetheless, and I would really have loved to see him stay another two or three years to see where he could take us. He just wasn't at the club long enough to be considered one of the all-time greats."

But Postecoglou did bring trophies and entertainment back to Celtic Park at a crucial moment. For that, he will be fondly remembered.

In his own words, "My ambition was always to give our fans a team they could be proud of, a team people talked about, and I think we have achieved that.

"Celtic is a phenomenal football club, and so much more—and I will forever be a supporter of this great institution. I wish everyone connected with Celtic nothing but continued success."

CHAPTER 16
From a Trickle to a Flood

In 2006, Australia qualified for its first World Cup finals in 32 years. The majority of the players that travelled to Germany were at European clubs, but the squad did not feature any Scotland-based or Scottish-born players. Mark Viduka and Craig Moore did provide an interest for Celtic and Rangers fans, while Hibs fans could have caught a glimpse of a young Mark Milligan—12 years before he found his way to Edinburgh.

The picture was similar four years later. At the 2010 World Cup in South Africa, Moore was soldiering on at the age of 34, while Milligan was again selected. Defender David Carney had a brief and unmemorable stint at Hamilton Academical on his CV but, again, there were no players based in Scotland.

The absence of players who plied their trade in Scotland continued in 2014. This time Ryan McGowan was the player with the strongest connection, having been at Hearts as recently as 2013, following five years at the club. Matt McKay's forgettable spell at Rangers barely registers. Adam Taggart would have a similarly unremarkable spell at Dundee United the following year.

This Australia team was managed by future Celtic boss Ange Postecoglou, but that was still seven years away. So at this point, links to the national side existed but they were few and not always strong.

Things then started to change.

In 2018, Tom Rogic, of Celtic, was central to the hopes of the Australian side. Jamie Maclaren, of Hibs, was also in the squad as was the man whose formative years were spent with Scottish clubs—Jackson Irvine. Mark Milligan was selected again, as was former St Mirren and future Celtic midfielder Aaron Mooy.

In 2022, six players plying their trade in the Scottish Premiership made it into Australia's World Cup squad. A further five had played or would go on to play in Scotland's top tier. Jason Cummings, Martin Boyle and Harry Souttar were all born in Scotland and grew up there, connecting to Australia through a parent.

This surging interest in Australian players has several causes, but there has been incredible change from the early struggles of Dave Mitchell, Will Hastie and Lachlan Armstrong, through the big successes of Craig Moore, Tony Vidmar, Mark Viduka and Scott McDonald, to the solid if less spectacular careers of the likes of Danny Invincibile and Ryan McGowan.

The successes have encouraged more clubs to put their trust in Aussie players and investigate the market. Looking for reasons for the high degree of interest among Scottish clubs, the responses are various, but there are certain consistent points raised by a number of those in the know.

Scott McDonald said, "I think Scottish people identify with the work ethic in Australians, which is what they like and respect. I think budgets have a lot to do with it as clubs try to find a diamond in the rough. Hearts have done that really well in their recruitment, and that highlights that there are good players playing in Australia.

"Numerous Australians have come through the doors of Scottish football and made a really huge impact. I think it's down to our work ethic and the way that the two cultures collide. I always found the Scots were my type of people, and vice versa, and we can integrate very quickly into Scottish ways and football. Scottish people respect you for what you're willing to put out there."

Tony Vidmar believes it's not necessarily what the Aussies love about Scotland but about what the Scots love about the Aussies.

He said, "The coaches and the sporting directors love the Aussie mentality. They never complain about anything, they just get on with the job. I think we've got some good quality players over there now. And Australia's a bit of a cheap market at this point. I think a lot of clubs see an opportunity to bring in a player for a relatively small transfer fee, and maybe in three to four years' time, they can sell him on for a lot more money.

"You know what you're going to get from Aussie players, and from an Australian point of view, it's a good league to get into because you know that you'll probably play. It's a smart move for Scottish sides to pick up Aussie players. In the next few years, maybe the Australian players will become too expensive for the Scottish market, but for the time being, it's definitely a relationship that's good for both sides."

Ahead of the 2022 World Cup, Paul Williams wrote an article for *The Guardian* titled 'How the Socceroos' World Cup hopes are underpinned by ties with Scotland'. In the article, he wrote:

"There has always been a strong connection between the two countries, given the deep colonial roots of modern Australia, especially when it comes to football."

Talking to me in 2024, he again highlighted the cultural links as he said, "There are deep historical connections between Australia and Scotland. In a football sense, there has always been a sense of Britishness to the game in Australia and so many players with Scottish heritage have represented the national team.

"Scottish clubs have always appreciated the style and attitude of Australian players. They seem to adapt well to Scottish football. The success Ange had has probably shone even more of a spotlight on Australian players.

"A large number of players over the years have had success in Scottish football, so I think clubs have become interested in Australian players. And a lot of Aussie players are now looking at Scotland as a destination to make a career."

However, Williams also recognises a more pragmatic side to the popularity of Scotland. While the Australian sides of the 2000s could call on several players in Europe's 'Big Five' leagues, that is no longer the case.

Williams added, "Another reason why players are looking to Scotland is simply that Australia's player development pathways are not what they once were. We're not sending players to the highest levels of the game anymore, so we have to look at alternative options in Europe to start their careers.

"They have to look at leagues outside the top tier of European football. Scotland fits the bill. There's an easy cultural exchange, the language is English and the football style is similar. Australian players are attractive to Scottish clubs and Scottish clubs are attractive to Australian players at the same time."

For many years, the sporting traditions of Australia have made them relative over-achievers in international competition. Danny Lennon feels that this development of sports people in Australia helps them to adapt in Scotland.

He said, "The players in Australia are athletes before they're football players because their sports science is way ahead of us. We're using it a lot better here now, but Australia had a head start.

"The players that are coming over are well suited to the demands of the Scottish game and its fast and furious pace. I also think that the Australian players had to come over because there's limited scouting of the A-League and they see it as a platform that could act as a stepping stone to other leagues in Europe. There's some great work done behind the scenes to identify these talents."

However, back at the beginning of the tentative steps taken by Australians in the Scottish game, it was nothing to do with scouting or finding bargain buys. It was more of a family affair.

Will Hastie highlights how many players like him, and Dave Mitchell before him, ended up in Scottish football mainly because of the fathers who pushed them in that direction.

He said, "I think our traits have always been really well aligned with Scottish football—really competitive, disciplined, physical and never beaten. If you look at the ones that made it in Scotland, they're some of the toughest competitors Australia has ever produced. I think the football style suited Australians.

"But don't underestimate how much the Scottish diaspora influenced Australian football. A lot of relatives, a lot of fathers came from descendants of Scots and it was quite natural for some of them to go back to Scotland and play.

"I think right now, for all the Australian players in the Scottish league, it's a really good stepping stone from the A-League to European football for those that have the dream to make the journey. I just think the football fits logically as a nice progression for a young player who might have come through the Australian youth system and started in the A-League.

"I think Scottish football is doing a really good job of developing young Australian talent. It seems to suit the players really well."

Lachlan Armstrong, another player who has his father to thank for pushing him towards Scotland, broadly agrees with his old mate Will.

He said, "I guess it seems like a reasonable step between the A-League and English football. I believe from recent discussions, it's easier in terms of getting the work permit. If a young Australian gets into Scotland and then gets a few caps under their belt for the Socceroos, it makes it easier to make the step up to England.

"From a football level, it's somewhere in between. So for any young footballer wanting to make that step into European football, it's a good place to be because it's a slight step up, but it's manageable.

"I think the Aussie culture fits in quite well in Scotland, so it's a comfortable place for people to live and enjoy life as well as their football."

Football is cyclical and often based on trends. As recently as the 2019-20 season, just five Australian players were plying their trade in the Scottish Premiership. In the COVID-affected 2020–21 campaign, it dropped to three. The total reached seven in 2021–22, a season that also witnessed the addition of the first Aussie manager.

There was then a jump to 15 in 2022–23—the season in which six were selected for the Socceroos World Cup squad. The number dropped by just one in 2023–24, though 15 again if you include Mark Birighitti's seven-day emergency loan at Kilmarnock. There was a drop to 11 at the start of the 2024–25 season, though that did not include Marco Tilio, on loan at Melbourne City from Celtic.

Of course, not all of the many Aussies to play in Scotland's top tier have made much of an impact. Several have been peripheral, at best, and a number have stayed just one year or enjoyed a short loan spell. For every Moore, there has been a Milligan and for every Rogic, a Tilio.

However, as this book has demonstrated, a large number of Australians have settled and adapted and, if current trends continue, Scotland will remain an attractive destination for Australian players who want to follow in the footsteps of some of the finest players the country has produced.

And for Scottish fans, they have given so much back. From Vidmar's goal against Parma to McDonald's goal against AC Milan. From Moore's titanic battles with Larsson to McGowan's strike against Hibs. There have been the countless moments of genius produced by Rogic and Jackson Irvine leading Ross County to their first-ever major honour.

Whatever comes next, the achievements of many Socceroos in Scotland ensure that their place in the country's football history is secure.

Acknowledgements

Many thanks to the contributors who gave up their free time to help provide content for the book. In no particular order, they are: Tony Vidmar, Paul Lambert, Scott McDonald, Danny Invincibile, Danny Lennon, Erik Paartalu, Will Hastie, Lachlan Armstrong, Dave McPherson, Dylan McGowan, Dave Mitchell, Jason Dasey, Hamish Carton, Joel Sked, Patrick McPartlin, Paul Williams. The time these guys gave up to talk to me was very much appreciated.

Thanks also to those who helped or tried their best to help put me in touch with contributors, including Bonita Mersiades, Jason Dasey (again), Paul Boyle, Mark Hamill, Michael Sheridan, Pablo Muniz and Michael Martin.

It was a long journey from pitching the idea to completion, and it depended on assistance from a number of people. A special mention to LinkedIn, without which some of the interviews would not have been possible.

Paul Murphy
July 2025

More really good football books from Fair Play Publishing

Encyclopedia of Matildas
Beyond the World Cup 2023

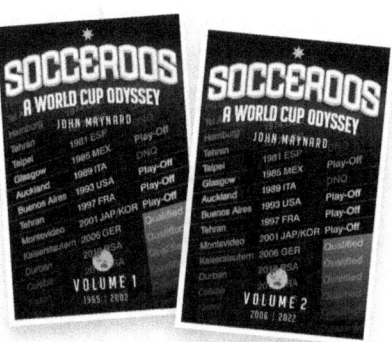
Socceroos – A World Cup Odyssey,
1965 to 2022 Volumes 1 and 2

Noddy, The Untold Story
of Adrian Alston

"Get Your Tits Out
for the Lads"

Hear Us Roar
– An anthology of
emerging women
football writers

When Mum and Dad
See Me Kick

Football Fans
In Their Own Write...

Available from
fairplaypublishing.com.au/shop
and all good bookstores

fairplaypublishing.com.au

www.ingramcontent.com/pod-product-compliance
Lightning Source LLC
Chambersburg PA
CBHW052032070526
44584CB00016B/2009